For Barbara & David
With love & thanks for your supp~

Paul

THE TREASURER'S CHALLENGE – 2018

This edition first published in July 2018

Paul Stuart asserts his right to be identified as the editor of this work under the Copyright, Designs and Patents Act 1988.

ISBN: 9780244098018

THE TREASURER'S CHALLENGE – 2018

FOREWORD

This book is the result of a challenge which involved individuals taking a £10 note from our Treasurer. It's not normal for a Treasurer to dole out money, but she took the risk and added a stern instruction that those who took the challenge had to make the money grow. The idea, of course, derives from the parable of the talents in the New Testament. The talent as a unit of value meant 'gift' or 'skill' in English and other languages. An Egyptian talent, however, had monetary worth.

My response to the challenge was to ask the congregation of St. Piran's Church, Perranarworthal, Cornwall to contribute written pieces with the intention of compiling and publishing a book. It was my hope that the book could then be purchased, thereby increasing the original sum for the benefit of the church.

You are holding the result in your hands. It contains prose, poetry, personal stories, both true and imaginary, non-fiction and a wealth of social history and information that will, no doubt, be a lasting legacy for those involved and their families and friends.

I have had to keep some identities secret at the request of the people involved. The reasons are complex and varied, but I'll take them to my grave, even though I am sorely tempted to kiss and tell. I have also had to make difficult editorial decisions about what to keep in and what to exclude. I hope nobody has felt slighted by this, but there may well be scope for another such effort in the future.

The poet John Milton worried about the limitations of his own gifts and achievements, even though he really should not have.

"When I consider how my light is spent
Ere half my days, in this dark world and wide,
And that one Talent, which is death to hide,
Lodg'd with me useless, though my Soul more bent

THE TREASURER'S CHALLENGE – 2018

To serve therewith my Maker, and present
My true account, lest he, returning, chide."

It has been a privilege to produce this book. I hope you enjoy it and are as amazed as I have been at the incredible range of talent and experiences that have been highlighted by this exercise. It has confirmed my long-held belief that there is a story behind every front door and the talent to tell it, if only we came out from behind its protection. Perhaps we'll do another one!

Paul Stuart, Church Warden, July 2018.

THE TREASURER'S CHALLENGE – 2018

DEDICATION

PERSONAL STORIES

POETRY CORNER

THE INTELLECTUAL SECTION

DEDICATION

This book is dedicated to my late wife Jan, who died on June 5th 2018 in tragic circumstances after a fall on the Chapter House steps of Truro Cathedral two days earlier. She was the light of my life and I miss her dreadfully. I am fortunate to be surrounded by the love of friends and family who keep me going, and without whom my darkness would be intolerable. I shall be forever in their debt. In particular, Canon Simon Bone has been an absolute rock. He is everything a good shepherd should be and much, much more.

The first contribution is a poem which was written the day after Jan passed and was beautifully read at her Cremation Service by the poet herself. Thank you Rosemary.

THE TREASURER'S CHALLENGE – 2018

<u>FOR JAN</u>

Bright soul
Gently glowing
Like a candle
With your soft voice and shining eyes
And little acts of kindness
Sharing warmth.

So smart
Elegant and radiant
In your vibrant colours
Like a Festal candle
Bright as your smile
Bringing cheer.

Then, in an instant
In a heartbeat
Everything was changed
As your friends stood, shocked and silent,
Your soft flame flickered,
Flickered,
And was gone.

And we, left in sudden darkness
From which your gentle radiance has fled,
Slowly begin to realise
That what we have, too briefly, witnessed
Was not a candle
But a shooting star.

Rosemary Aitken

THE TREASURER'S CHALLENGE – 2018

MY FIRST STAY IN HOSPITAL

At the tender age of ten I had to go into hospital in London. In those days children were often parked amongst adults and I ended up in a men's ward. My appendix was removed and so was some of my innocence. At the time we lived quite a way from the hospital, so visits were difficult, especially as I had a younger sister who wasn't allowed in. I remember being torn between thoughts of relief because I wouldn't have to tolerate her constant chatter and homesickness because I loved my family and missed being at home.

I didn't think it usual to be in such a place for something as mundane as an appendectomy, but I'd had a heart problem from birth and thus it was deemed necessary to place me in a specialist hospital on a men's ward. Not unnaturally my fellow patients all seemed ancient to me and loneliness gripped me very quickly. I felt small and vulnerable. That feeling was certainly not eased when I looked around the ward and took stock.

Directly opposite was a grey haired individual who hawked, hacked and spat his way through my first day. Granted he used a receptacle, but I'd never seen nor heard anything like it in my life. On his left from my viewpoint was a thin bony skeleton which hardly seemed to move. His eyes, which were sunken into his completely bald skull, also never seemed to move. He had a sort of fixed, glazed stare. I did spot him move his arm once, but that was just to pick his nose. To the right of the hacking man lay a grizzly bear. He was massive and had tubes and pipes appearing from every conceivable orifice and wires strapped everywhere else. I remember he moaned and groaned a lot, but nobody seemed to take any notice, so he just continued anyway. Looking back, I think he gained some relief just by doing that.

THE TREASURER'S CHALLENGE – 2018

Beside me in the bed to my right there resided a most peculiar person. Or so it seemed to me. I couldn't keep looking at him because I was old enough to have learned not to stare for fear of giving offence or causing trouble. However, it is human nature to take in one's surroundings and I wanted to make sure I was safe! He was probably not very old and may have been a perfectly nice man, but he unsettled me by staring back. Surely, I thought, he must know it is rude to stare, but he just kept doing it. His eyes were a piercing blue; he had a mop of jet black hair on his head and much more of the same on his chest. He had no tubes or wires and so could move freely whenever the fancy took him, which it did quite often. I noticed that he visited every patient that I could see from my bed and talked in hushed tones to each. After such a visitation each bedbound recipient would be agitated and call for urgent assistance. Thankfully he never visited me, presumably because he thought it not so much of a challenge to upset a small boy, but I kept an eye on him.

Immediately to my left was a middle aged chatty man. He was quietly spoken, read his newspaper and his book and offered me sweets. I liked him. The first night was very frightening and I tried not to sleep until I was sure everybody else was asleep first. I reasoned I would be safer that way. The plan didn't work. The hacking man did not sleep at all; he just carried on with his noisy, juicy expectorations and nobody came to check on him. The nurses had no need of a bedside alarm for him because they knew that if he went quiet they should come running. Skeleton Man, to his credit, moved even less at night. I think he was rehearsing for the time when he would close those staring eyes for the last time.

However, he woke on my first morning, picked his nose as usual, and just lay there waiting patiently for the day to unfold. Grizzly actually slept all night, although I still don't know how. He snored and roared his way through the night, with his tubes and wires bouncing around and upon him. Again, the nurses paid him no heed, presumably employing the same principal as they did for Hacking Man. Old Blue Eyes was actually strapped to his bed at night. He had obviously made too many visitations and the nurses didn't want to be disturbed.

Actually, I realise now that the way each patient was treated at night was individually tailored to ensure the nurses were not needed at all. Very clever, I thought. My chatty, book-reading friend to my left was the man who discovered the real reason for this and shared his secret finding with me. He had, he told me before lights out, discovered that the doctors and nurses were playing a real life game of the same name during the wee small hours and made every possible arrangement not to be interrupted. Why my newly found friend should think a ten-year-old would be enriched by this knowledge I couldn't say, but it had a profound effect for years to come.

My operation took place on the second day of my stay. I don't remember much about it as I was asleep at the time. I was grateful for this because I had not slept at all on that first night. When I eventually awoke, I noticed an empty bed across the ward and asked my chatty friend about it. He looked at me morosely and said that Skeleton Man had picked his nose for the last time and was no more. I didn't respond, but remember thinking that I wouldn't like to be the next person to take up residence in that particular bed.

One incident that amused me happened on my fourth morning. By that time, I had been allowed out of bed. Nowadays they boot you out of bed just a few hours after surgery, presumably because they don't want you getting used to the good life of doing nothing, eating their delicious food and making a nuisance of yourself. On that morning the doctor, accompanied by the terrifying

Matron, stopped at the hacking man's bed and in a voice loud enough for all to hear declared that cigarettes were the cause of his condition, it was not going to improve and would almost certainly kill him. He went on to advise anybody who was listening, which was everybody in the entire ward, if not the entire hospital, that smoking was sinful and he resented treating patients who ruined their own lives by practicing such a filthy habit. Moreover, he railed, he would in future think twice about treating people who damaged themselves in that way. That was quite a radical thing to do in those days, but he has turned out to be quite a forward thinker. Anyway, when he and Matron had swept away in a cloud of disgruntlement, a few of us gathered on the balcony to get some much needed fresh air. The balcony overlooked the street and the front entrance to the hospital. On the opposite side of the road we could see a sweetshop, which obviously also sold newspapers, magazines and cigarettes. We watched with mild disinterest as people came and went, but our attention was caught by our eminent heart surgeon striding into the shop. He reappeared a few minutes later with a paper tucked under his arm and stopped on the pavement. He removed something from his pocket, put it to his mouth and lit it. With obvious satisfaction he drew a deep breath before exhaling a cloud of blue smoke. This drew a round of applause from our balcony and, after looking up at his cheering patients, he scuttled away in deep embarrassment. Skeleton Man would have smiled if he could.

Ironically the surgeon had been correct in his analysis and Hacking Man passed away that night. That meant that two of my fellow inmates had been taken by the grim reaper and it was only my fifth day. This set me thinking and I realised that if the attrition rate continued at the same pace, it wouldn't be long before my number was called. Unfortunately, I had been told that I would not be due for release until at least ten days after my operation. I have to admit that I showed signs of panic. After all, I calculated, I therefore had to somehow survive for the best part of another week and there weren't that many patients left on the ward in front of me in the queue. Of course, I was relying on the fact that we would be taken in strict order of admittance, but I couldn't depend on that. When my mother visited me that afternoon I managed to persuade her that I would be available for release within two days. She was doubtful, but between us we managed to cajole the surgeon and Matron to agree to the plan, with the proviso that I could walk properly, that my eating and toiletry habits had been returned to normal and that I would return to have stitches removed on what would have been the tenth day of being an inmate.

I was overjoyed, not least because it reduced the chances of my maker catching up with me in hospital. He may have had other plans for me elsewhere, but at least I was giving him a run for his money. My plan was further vindicated when I awoke the next morning to the news that Grizzly had been taken during the night. Apparently, even the plethora of tangled tubes, pipes and wires had not saved him. This worried me greatly because I realised that if all those accoutrements had not been able to save him, then what chance did I have with no attachments to protect me? I never did find out what his problem was.

Thus, six days and five nights had elapsed and three fellow patients had disappeared. Even my ten-year old maths could work out that it was imperative my escape plan worked. When I awoke on my sixth morning I was staggered to learn that all of my previous day's companions were still present and correct, despite the fact that the Grim Reaper had, up to this point, been most active during the hours of darkness. I now reasoned, with child-like innocence, that the odds had been tilted back in my favour a little.

By this time, I was able to walk reasonably well, although the stitches pulled uncomfortably. Toiletry habits were returning to normal, or as normal as possible given the awful hospital food with which we were provided. I had discussed my plan with Chatty Man and he ventured that I was being very sensible because if the law of averages in the ward didn't get you then the food would. He admitted that he had noticed the mortality rate and was very worried because he was next in line.

As it turned out he was wrong. Chatty Man and I had noticed that my neighbour with the blue eyes, who was strapped to his bed each night, had not had his bindings removed that day and was very still indeed. As there were no monitors with tell-tale beeps that hover over each patient as is the norm nowadays, nobody could tell whether he had just decided to continue sleeping in order to avoid the perils of breakfast or something more sinister had happened. It was mid-morning by the time a diligent nurse took some notice and discovered his unblinking blue eyes gazing up at the ceiling.

Curtains were hastily drawn around his bed, which, apart from cutting off my view, was also rather unfriendly, and several other nurses and Matron scuttled into that sanctum. A senior looking doctor appeared and I heard him make an authoritative pronouncement to the assembled crowd. I didn't catch what he actually said, but the meaning was clear from his low rumbling tone. Curtains were then drawn around everybody's beds, which annoyed us all as the developing drama had become the highlight of the day and we wanted to see what happened next.

As if by magic, when our curtains were removed, Strapped Down Man had disappeared and a freshly made bed stood there, inviting its next victim with its crisp white sheets, neatly turned down to resemble a toothless maw topped by a perfectly laundered pillowed headstone. Being only ten years old I didn't know where hospitals put dead bodies, so I imagined another ward which was gradually being filled by my erstwhile companions. I confided to my chatty friend that I thought they wouldn't take much looking after and that at least they were avoiding the hospital food, but he didn't seem to find that funny and returned to his newspaper for quite some time.

There wasn't much time for anything else to happen because I was let out the next day.　　　　Paul Stuart

THE TREASURER'S CHALLENGE – 2018

HAPPINESS COMES IN SMALL DOSES

I was born on January 30th, 1938 in Richmond, Yorkshire. My father was in the Royal Signals Regiment based at Catterick Camp. My sister Anne was 4 and my brother David was 9. In 1939 my father was posted to the North West Frontier in India, now the border between Pakistan and Afghanistan. Shortly after my Father arrived my Mother, my Sister and I followed by boat to India. David was left in England with an Aunt to continue his education.

The second world war broke out on the 1st September 1939 and soon after my Father was posted to Singapore. He became a Japanese prisoner of war when Singapore was invaded by the Japanese in February 1942. As a result of this my Mother, my Sister and I were stuck in India because we were not allowed to go back to England. We did not return to England until around Easter 1945, just before the war in Europe ended.

I have so many happy memories of India in these intervening years and I would like to share some of them with you. Obviously, because of my age, then and now, my memories are rather disjointed but nevertheless remain very vivid.

For the five intervening years we were looked after by the British Army and moved from one army base to another in India. Because of the Indian climate we moved up to hill stations in the north and south in the spring, and then down to the plains in the autumn ready for the winter. This involved railway journeys of 2 or 3 days through beautiful scenery. Looking out of the carriage window I saw elephants pulling tree trunks in the woods and buffalo ploughing fields. I remember the stations where we could get off to have meals and buy bananas galore, and there were trees growing on the platforms. In the evening I would snuggle down on the top bunk for the night and listen to the clickity click of the moving train. I thought it was glorious.

Some summers we went up to Ninitahl, a hill station in the Himalayas. It had been built in the crater of an extinct volcano and was beautiful. It had a large lake in the bottom and snow on the tops of the surrounding high mountains. The Himalayas are massive and go on up and up into the sky where you see white peaks appear way above the tops of the clouds. Here we had the ground floor of a house which we shared with a collection of animals, such as monkeys, snakes and birds, centipedes and scorpions, which seemed to come into the house whenever they liked. The bathroom had a tin bath sitting in a leaded area with a geyser with which to heat the water and which went off like a bomb if you were not careful. The leaded area had a larger hole to let the bathwater out with a grill on it. The trouble was that cobras and grass snakes pushed up the grill and came in. We had to go on a snake hunt before having a bath. We had a handy wooden stick to kill them if they did not return the way they'd come in, which they usually did. We had a strict rule to cope with the effects of scorpions and centipedes: always shake your shoes out before you put them on. I still do that. My friend, Judy, who lived upstairs, woke up one morning to find she had a 'centipede crawl', which are poisonous scratches on her arm. This made her very ill. We always had mosquito nets on our beds. The army poured petrol on the ponds and still water surfaces and set light to it at the breeding time to kill the larvae. The monkeys were everywhere and enjoyed sitting on the veranda around the house. We left them alone and they left us alone, but they were always ready for scraps of food.

I went to a convent school in Ninitahl, which was across the valley from our house. I went there on a pony being led by a man. The trouble was that the path through the woods going down to the lake had tree roots across it, which the pony would mistake for a snake and buck me off. Not much appreciated by a five/six - year old. I learned nothing at the convent but the first verse of 'Lavender Blue Dilly Dilly,' which I had to recite at a school concert. Whilst I was at the Convent my sister was at the Hallet War School further up the mountains with fantastic views across the Himalayas. It is now one of the top boys' schools.

Our house was up a twisting road looking down on the lake and up to the high mountains. On one corner of the road down to the town a man spent the day roasting peanuts on a fire and for a few Annas I got a bagful. Lovely. The only way to eat Peanuts.

We had a Bearer, Head Servant, who wore a white turban, He called me the chota, chota sahib (little, little mister). I thought he was great and he used to take me for long walks in the woods up the hills behind the house, pointing out animal tracks, birds' nests, porcupine tracks and quills and other interesting things. There was even a black panther's foot print on one occasion. I remember sitting outside our kitchen with a group of Indians who were smoking a Hubble Bubble. This was a container, heated on a fire, which allowed opium and tobacco fumes to be drawn through hot water. Several people could use it at the same time. At that time, I spoke very good Hindustani and my Mother used to use me as an interpreter. I was never shown anything but kindness by the Indians, although I suspect I was a pain in the neck a lot of the time. Our Bearer stayed with us during several years of our stay in India and always looked after me as if he was my father. Many, many happy times were spent with him.

As winter approached we used to leave Ninitahl in the north or Ooti Hill Station in the south for warmer climes in the plains. More train journeys, especially the lovely Nilgiri Hill Railway up to Ooti, as seen on TV. I have very few memories of Outi and what I do have has been muddied by the TV programmes. India is the most beautiful, vast, changing country, where everything is huge. Mountains, open spaces, plains, rivers a mile or so wide which the train crossed on steel bridges. I still have a deep rooted need to be in the mountains, which is why we bought a cottage 600 feet up in the Snowdonia National Park, which, sadly, I sold after my wife died. Many, many happy times spent there.

We stayed at Lahore in the plains for the winter. I have a vivid memory of Miss Christie's Hotel. She was an elderly lady, by comparison to me, who used to serve me with grey boiled brains. She said they were good for me, but I refused to eat them. You should try them, they are disgusting. To add to my misery, she used to play the piano to me as I sat all on my own in the huge dining room. Eventually she gave up the task. I have never eaten brains since.

The Indians were very keen on showing off in grand style and once we watched a procession with a Maharaja sitting on the huge, brightly decorated seat with a sunshade arrangement on an elephant. He was followed by a procession of people, all in bright clothes. I have no idea who he was, but Maharajas were heads of various areas and very wealthy.

One year we all got whooping cough and were sent to Srinagar in northern India, now in the disputed Pakistan and India area and very difficult to visit. Yet another spectacularly beautiful place. Because we had whooping cough we had to stay on a house boat on the lake. It was a lovely, large wooden houseboat with carved wooden panels. The servants stayed in another house boat attached to the stem and then to the lake bank. Snakes were everywhere in the water. We had a lovely English girl with us to look after us. She used to take me for walks along the edge of the lake and I remember her explaining why it was that the moon seemed to stay the same distance away from us even though we were walking towards it. I was quite sure it should be getting closer. It is amazing what trivial things stay in the mind of a five or six- year old. Various films like, 'Passage to India', show the same houseboats.

My father used to write letters to us when he was allowed to. He wrote all his news in the letters which had to be passed by the Japanese and they blacked out everything they did not want us to know about. However, if one held the letter against a window, what was written underneath the blacked out portion could be seen.

During our stay in India we had two very good Army friends, known to me as Uncle Douglas, an Army doctor, and Uncle Robin, who was in the Royal Engineers. Uncle Douglas used to make wooden model aeroplanes for me and it was always a very exciting time when he came to stay and produced a bomber or fighter. Toys were almost non-existent. Uncle Robin used to take me to the Royal Engineer's exhibitions, which they put on every now and then. I loved watching the huge tractors, excavators and other pieces of army equipment being demonstrated at work. It was a real treat.

We moved to Poona, a large army base about fifty miles from Bombay (now known as Mumbai), shortly before we left India and one day, as a treat, the bearer took me to the railway station. I was standing on the station platform when a loco stopped just alongside me and the driver started talking and asked me if I would like to go on to the footplate, which I did. Thrills. He also asked if I would like to go for a ride but I said no. More fool me, as he was only going to do some shunting in the station and then he came back. There was also a shoe maker near where we lived and I used to go and watch them making shoes. The Army camp had a large swimming pool, and friends taught me how to swim. Also to ride a bike.

Eventually the War was coming to an end and we got a passage home. It took us five weeks by sea in a convoy. I used to watch the other ships and there was always something happening, even if it was only the ship's propellers coming out of the water in a rough sea. In such seas I would sit up on deck as it was easier not to be seasick there. My mother seemed to spend her time playing endless Mah Jong and I sometimes joined in. We were on the SS Orion, which was a troop ship and I used to go down to their cinema and watch films with them. We were attacked on two occasions. I remember one by air and once by torpedo. They missed. We came through the Suez Canal and into the Mediterranean Sea. When we got to Malta all the passengers had to go on deck and the crew issued life jackets and moved us around so that the boat was upright in order that it would clear the submarine nets spread across the harbour entrance. There were many naval ships in the harbour, which was completely bombed and in ruins. This was my first site of what war could do and it made a great impression on me. When we had been re-fuelled we sailed from Malta back to the UK but had to go to Glasgow, as it was too dangerous to go up the Channel.

There had been a case of small pox on the ship, so we all had to get a jab as we left the ship and got on to the train for London. As we approached London the lights went out because of the blackout. We arrived at Kings Cross in the dark and were put into army trucks with little slitted head lamps and taken to Marylebone station. Here I met my brother, in the dark, for the first time. He was 16 and nine years older than me. We arrived at our destination and got in a taxi, still in darkness, to my Grandfather's house.

The next day was cold and I was in the garden with only thin clothes on. My grandfather came out of the house with a coat for me. It was around Easter 1945. We stayed with my grandparents for a while but then moved to a flat over two garages. It had very little room and my sister and I were sent to nearby boarding schools.

THE TREASURER'S CHALLENGE – 2018

My father arrived back in England after being released as a POW on the 31st October, 1945. One day, my father came to fetch me from school and this was the first time I had seen him. It's is a very strange sensation when, at the age of seven, you meet you father for the first time. Soon after that I went with him to Heathrow, then a military base, and he was issued with new uniform and civilian clothes. He was soon posted to BOAR Control Commission in Germany, to release the concentration camps. Only the army would do that.

Happiness comes in small but very precious doses. It certainly did for me.

Tony Woodbridge.

THE TREASURER'S CHALLENGE – 2018

A TRUE STORY

When I was born, in a nursing home south of London, medical science was not as advanced as it is today. As a result, the doctor who attended my birth told my parents that their child did not have any chance of living. I had been born with an exomphalos, caused by a weakness in the abdominal wall attached to the umbilical cord.

My father, however, had other ideas. He organised a taxi and I was driven to St. Thomas' Hospital in London, where I was baptised on the day I was born and where he was told that the diagnosis that he had been given at the nursing home was accurate and that nothing could be done for his child. Another taxi ride through London to St. George's Hospital resulted in the same medical judgment.

Finally, there was a third taxi ride to Great Ormond Street Hospital. There, a surgeon told my father that he was prepared to operate but that his child had only a one in a million chance of surviving.

The operation was successful. A further operation took place when this child was four years old and the last operation at the age of ten. Only then was I allowed to participate in any kind of sport.

All three operations were carried out by the same surgeon, who, research has revealed [via Google], had played rugby for England in 1910, was surgeon to our royal family and to other European royal families and had been knighted. His name – Sir Lancelot Barrington-Ward, whose father had been rector of Duloe in Cornwall and a canon of Truro Cathedral.

To him and to a very determined father, I owe my life.

I still attend St. Piran's Church, Perranarworthal.

The lesson from this is: If at first you don't succeed, try, try and try again.

Anon.

THE TREASURER'S CHALLENGE – 2018

ALL THINGS THAT CREEP AND CRAWL

In the 50s we lived in a mining town in what was Northern Rhodesia. Every other year we would go on holiday for a long stay on my grandmother's farm in South Africa. The distance we had to travel was 1385 miles and took 5 days. On day one mum and dad and we three girls set out to Ndola, by car where we would board the train. This was a longish drive on very bad roads in a little ford Anglia, packed to the gunnels with two adults, three children, luggage for a six week stay and food for the journey. At Ndola the car was loaded onto the train, and we found our compartment and settled in.

My mother had a constant war on 'germs' and there was much wiping of surfaces with water and Dettol. It was always exciting sleeping on the train. The stewards arrived and arranged the compartment to have three bunks on each side, which were quickly and expertly made up into comfortable beds with immaculate white sheets and navy blue blankets. In the morning the same stewards came and packed up the bedding, putting it into huge canvas bags marked with the compartment number. My father always said South African Railways, was mentioned in The Bible: you know the piece .....God made all creatures that creep and crawl.

The day passed slowly. It was very hot, and there was an endless vista of African bush. We ate sandwiches, played games looked out of the window got smuts in our eyes, and generally became very grubby. The next night our bedding was brought to the compartment, beds made up and so to bed!

The next day always seemed the longest, still very hot, endless bush, and the train puffing on, but late that evening we arrived in Bulawayo. This was a high point, especially for my mother, because available on the station were bathrooms. These were huge rooms with big white enamel baths on huge ball and claw feet, masses of piping hot water, huge piles of fluffy white towels, a small bar of soap all for 2/6d! We all had baths, children were put into pyjamas and slippers and onto another train, with new beds already made up.

The next day was very exciting. We crossed the magnificent Victoria Falls at a snail's pace. I always thought it was to give the passengers a chance to see the thundering waters, but an engineer uncle said it was to give the bridge a chance. At Victoria Falls station a family friend was always there to say a quick hello. She supplied us with yet more sandwiches, hardboiled eggs and oranges. Eventually we arrived at Mafeking. This was, and I imagine still is, a very, very dusty place. Dad went to see about off-loading the car. All our luggage was loaded into the car and we set off to drive the last 275 miles to the farm.

We had wonderful holidays on the farm where my mother has been born, seeing our cousins, and there was lots of riding and playing tennis. After about six weeks we set off for home in Northern Rhodesia. Sometimes the trains were very delayed, up to hours, and even days. The excuses were very varied. One I liked best was "elephants on the line."

Jacqui Hopwood.

THE TREASURER'S CHALLENGE – 2018

A FAMILY HOLIDAY IN USA

U.S.A.
BUNCH BEACH, WHERE PICTURE WAS DONE

Every year for the past forty years I have visited my Cornish family in Fort Myers, Florida, apart from the numerous members who are buried at Mylor Churchyard and Illogan.

A few years ago, whilst in Florida with my son Marcus, we went to our favourite beach. Bunch Beach is a very deserted three-mile long area very close to the swamps. It is absolutely beautiful, with the backdrop of mango trees and shrub-land.

It was Easter time and I suddenly thought I would celebrate Jesus. I firstly drew a picture of Jesus in the sand. The eyes were shells and his eyebrows pieces of twig. The hair was so much sea weed from the beach. The backdrop of Bunch Beach provided the thorny crown which he bore. Finally, I collected four sticks to make a frame. Easter certainly came to this beach, as many passers-by took photos of my basic work. My son eventually told one man who admired the picture that his mother had done this and it was put onto YouTube. The tide came on daily, of course, and yet, strangely, the picture remained intact for over two weeks on its white sand setting. I was amazed that shells, twigs, sand and sea weed could give so much pleasure at Easter tide.

Gill Farnworth

THE TREASURER'S CHALLENGE – 2018

<u>MY GREAT CORNISH ADVENTURE – OR HOW I ARRIVED THERE!</u>

It was a cold winter. I was fifteen years old; a mere teenager in January 1954. Queen Elizabeth had been crowned in July 1953 and Hilary and Tensing had conquered Everest.

At last the world was at peace after the Second World War and there were promises of no more wars.

My father did it. He bought his first car, a 1939 Morris Eight Series 'E'. You know, the one with the rounded front and four doors. It cost him £190.00.
The luxuries included:

- No heater except for a black wire element, stuck on the windscreen.
- No proper headlights.
- Broken suspension
- Very doubtful drum brakes and a not very good handbrake.
- 4 forward gears and 1 reverse.
- No synchromesh on first gear.
- A starting handle, that you had to crank.
- A 4 stroke, side-valve engine.

He passed his driving test. We were on the road! Just. One of our first expeditions was to Wigan, which was a distance of 8 miles from our home in St. Helens, Lancashire. It was strong rugby league country, right next door to our deadly rivals at Wigan.

Setting off, we made a tentative approach to the centre of the town and the bobby controlling traffic on point duty. Confidently, we approached, with my father's hand pressed firmly on the windscreen indicating we wanted to go straight on. This was common practice in those days. He had a big smile on his face as my father wound the window down. Yes, it actually worked!

"Which one would you like, sir?" the policeman asked.

My father was taken aback. He didn't know what the man was talking about until he noticed that he had left his right trafficator out. This was, for a miraculous change, lit up. The other indicator was still stuck out, so there we were with both left and right trafficators out and my father indicating with his hand to go straight on. The trafficators never did return properly, and it needed a quick bang on the side of the door for them to drop back. My father proceeded, red faced, knowing the car must have looked like a plane about to take off.

Things did not always go smoothly in those days. Winter time was always difficult with our new acquisition. It wasn't kept in a garage. Quite often it refused to go. Could be plugs or points, battery, alternator etc. Anything.

As a raw 15-year-old who loved his sleep, getting up at 5.00 am or thereabouts was not my 'favourite fruit.' Turning out with my pj's under my trousers to get it started! With luck a swing of the starting handle would do the trick. At 15 and not yet with full adult strength, it needed a lot to 'turn over.' The alternative was pushing the car on the level to the top of a small hill to try and bump start it. In dry weather this was not too bad, but in winter it could be cold and wet with drops of freezing ice on the bodywork. If things worked well Dad would jump aboard, put into a higher gear and try the magic bump start. If that didn't work, and it often didn't, it was fiddle under the bonnet, phone the RAC or get a mechanic. That winter was our first experience of car ownership.

Summer, thankfully, arrived. Of course, there were no motorways in 1954, but a decision had been made. We would go to Newquay in Cornwall. An adventure. Lovely.

We loaded up. Dad was the only driver at that time, with this tremendous journey in front of him. We then had a AA route guide, which was something like a Satnav that didn't answer back. I remember that some of the directions were not easy to follow and I recall stopping for lunch and meeting two men with a vintage Renault car. They let us sit in and examine their car of which they were obviously proud. I've still got the photographs.

On and on we drove. It was endless. Dad was tired and we were still a long way from Newquay. We reached Porlock Hill. We knew about Lynmouth and Lynton and the flooding. We realised we were not going to reach Newquay in one day, so up Porlock Hill we went. As we approached what was a winding, extremely steep hill, we were already in first gear. We came to a sign that instructed us to engage a lower gear. Not a chance. Next we came to another sign that told of 'Danger to pedestrians; vehicles out of control.' We pressed on, going ever more slowly with each passing few feet. We were never going to reach the top. It was only the start of the hill! The footbrake was on and the handbrake pulled up as hard as my father could manage. Despite these sensible precautions we began to travel backwards, almost totally out of control.

At that point I jumped out and told my mother to do the same, just before the car disappeared into bushes at the side of the road. I remember, I think, the AA coming to the rescue. Later we found out that this hill was used for hill climbing events. We never, ever, reached the top. There are toll roads into and out of Lynmouth and Lynton and I now know why. The car was leaking oil and water as we limped into Lynmouth.

We stayed in a beautiful B&B. The damage done by the floods had largely been cleared by then.

Even using the toll roads, which were less steep but very winding, we needed at least two attempts to navigate the corners.

The holiday was now beginning in earnest. We stayed approximately two weeks. It was then that I began to realise what a beautiful place Cornwall is. We visited Newquay, Falmouth and Truro, where we went to the cathedral and signed the Register of Visitors, St. Austell, Mevagissey, Polperro, Looe and Carlyon Bay. I collected triangular flags from all these places.

We spent two nights in a Nissen half-round building in Carlyon Bay near the hotel. It's still there. My great uncle was caretaker of this hotel at that time. I was particularly struck by the fact that I was surrounded with barbed wire, even after the war. We joined in the Floral Dance in the streets and had a lovely holiday. Every minute was relished.

Returning home was less eventful. We managed to drive all the way until, at about midday and three miles from home on the East Lancashire Road, we hit trouble. Trundle! Trundle! Flat tyre. The spare wheel was, of course, at the bottom of the boot and everything had to come out. We eventually arrived home, weary but knowing we'd had a good holiday. We returned to Cornwall frequently and visited many places. All were great holidays.

Eventually, of course, all things change and family members spread their wings. Some went to Cornwall. My daughter spent approximately a year living and working in Probus and Lostwithiel, and by now was obviously going to settle in Cornwall. During her time there, I spent two weeks at Tregony on the Roseland Peninsular. We had, potentially, arrived. She settled in Ponsanooth with her family and friends and the time had come for me to make a move. Using the internet and a few visits, I began to examine areas and properties. It was like an ever growing mystery tour. I went to many places and eventually hit upon Perranwell, which I thought of as an outside chance. Guess what? A suitable house suddenly jumped out and hit me. Goal! Perranwell Station. My adventure was over. What a lovely place and what lovely people.   Gordon Denwood

THE TREASURER'S CHALLENGE – 2018

THE TREASURER'S CHALLENGE – 2018

AN EARLY EURO EXPERIENCE

The chance of being in at the birth of a new Parliament doesn't come around that often. Perhaps it was the attraction of swapping the life of a political correspondent of the Daily Telegraph for that of being the first MEP for Cornwall and Plymouth.

After three hectic weeks tearing about the new Euro constituency – Willie Whitelaw accurately but unintentionally described the campaign as "going around the country stirring up apathy – I was duly elected with a majority of 57,966. Quite pleased with that.

It was all new then. Perhaps it still is rather strange to the great British public nearly 40 years later when it looks likely that the UK's MEPs might become an extinct species.

Certainly for me it was a great culture shock. Everything was so different from Westminster, from the Chamber to the way of doing business. Foolishly, we thought we could change all that. We didn't.

True, we did introduce Question Time although the continentals made speeches rather than trying to pin down European Commissioners, and veteran Lord Harmer-Nicholls (he had the record for the most number of Commons election recounts) scored an immediate triumph of making Parliament meet on time. After a flourish of official lunches, there was a "no need to rush" drift back for the first working session. Only the Brits were in their seats in force on time. So, to the consternation of the officials, Harmer took the chair. He made his point.

Another of our members, a Biggles like retired senior RAF officer, took it upon himself to curb (unsuccessfully) a few old Italian practices. These included cheating by voting electronically for missing colleagues and signing for a day's expenses for them.

THE TREASURER'S CHALLENGE – 2018

A small group of us with same letter at the start of our surnames was christened "The H Bloc" by the Guardian newspaper because we took a hard line on the Parliament's expenditure. A small victory was defeating a proposal to strike gold medals for the founder members, the class of 1979.

But the biggest lesson we had to learn was that to get anywhere, alliances and compromises had to be made with other political groups. At the time the voting pattern seemed baffling. To our mutual embarrassment, someone worked out that at one time the two groups which had voted most often with each other were the British Conservatives and the Italian Euro Communists. They were much better dressed than we were and included one member of the Fiat family.

There was a pretty fair sprinkling of aristocrats in the initial Parliament. We had one or two but were outranked by the continentals. At one spell I sat in a hemi-cycle next to Otto van Habsburg. If history had been kinder, he would have been head of the Austro - Hungarian Empire. We also stayed in the same modest hotel in Strasbourg. At breakfast, his sons, (who were on his Parliamentary payroll) would bow, click their heels and wish Papa a good morning.

I'm in danger of giving the wrong impression. Yes, there were plenty of oddities about the Parliament. It was so frustrating for puritanical (or pompous if you prefer) Brits.

But there was also an underlying seriousness. I felt I did more for the fishing industry in my five years there than in my subsequent 14 years at Westminster. The same went for regional developments in Cornwall.

And it was fun. Not being a linguist I felt inadequate at times, and the Commons was my real home. But I would not have missed it for the world. Still, a gold medal for the grandchildren would have been nice!
David Harris.

THE TREASURER'S CHALLENGE – 2018

THE TREASURER'S CHALLENGE – 2018

<u>BERT</u>

Some years ago I was visiting someone at Tremorvah Residential Home in Redruth. Strangely enough, the building was once the nursing home where I first saw the light of day. There was there a very little old man who still had a sparkle in his eyes and whilst talking to him I asked the question. "Did you witness the eclipse in 1927?" Well, he had, and that was sufficient to start him off on what was a very interesting story which unfolded during successive visits.

Bert was born during the first World War and was living in a boy's home in East London. The regime was harsh and he was ill-treated. Permission had to be asked of older boys and staff for anything and everything. They cleaned, washed dishes and did many other menial tasks, and, should their endeavours not meet the standard required, they received the strap.

In 1929, at the age of thirteen, Bert and his mate, a fifteen-year-old boy, planned to escape. His mate, who was interested in sailing, made plans to stow away on a vessel leaving the port of London. The preparation was meticulous down to the sneaking of a newspaper from the home giving the shipping movements in and out of the port.

A typical early morning task for Bert and his mate was to push a barrow to the docks and there collect produce for the home from the warehouses under the supervision of an older boy. This happened before seven in the morning when the docks opened.

On the morning of the great escape an elder boy, accompanied by Bert and his mate, arrived at the docks by five to seven. It was still dark. His mate asked permission from the elder boy, addressed as "Sir", to go to the toilet. This was permitted on the strict understanding that he should be back within two minutes. Timidly, Bert asked permission to go too.

Permission was grudgingly granted with the two minutes' restriction also applying. After Bert's mate had studied the movements in and out of the port they decided on a Greek registered vessel for their dash to freedom. This was moored at a distance from the warehouse and was departing at seven twenty that morning. Therefore, as soon as they were out of sight of the senior boy, they made a dash in the dark and boarded the vessel. They were not spotted boarding as there was a considerable amount of hustle and bustle as the Greek vessel prepared to set sail. They then hid in a dirty locker in the fo'c'sle.

Bert's mate knew they had to stay well-hidden until the vessel was outside the three-mile limit, otherwise the captain would be compelled to return the stowaways to shore. The two boys knew ships had to keep to a three knot speed limit whilst within the three-mile zone, so according to their calculations they should be clear of the limit after three hours.

Cold, hungry and dirty the fateful time arrived for the boys to give themselves up. The bosun saw two frightened, cold and hungry boys standing before him. After looking them up and down he escorted them to the captain, who was more than bewildered. In front of him stood two dirty, smelly and poorly clothed youths. They gave the captain a truthful account of their predicament and burning desire to escape their harsh and horrible existence. Fortunately, the captain who spoke English believed the boys' story. He then instructed the bosun to get the boys washed, fed and clothed and then bring them back to see him. This was done. Bert was very small, in fact as a fully grow man he did not clear five feet and there was some difficulty in finding clean clothing to fit him as this had been provided by other members of the crew.

In front of the captain, Bert's mate was questioned as to what job he thought he could do on board. He felt that he had had good experience in the kitchens at the boy's home so the captain instructed the bosun to take him to the cook who would find him useful in the galley. When it came to Bert, the captain scratched his head and asked himself what on earth he could do with Bert on board. Bert said that he would like to work in the engine room as he was interested in steam and engines. Reluctantly the captain sent him off to the chief stoker.

Bert's time in the engine room turned out to be happy and rewarding. The stoker was a kindly man who wondered at first what he could do with this slip of a boy. The stoker made it clear that Bert was to follow his instructions and not do any more or any less than told. His job was to stoke the boilers. This proved difficult at first as the number eight shovel was bigger than Bert. However, with good instruction he learnt how to handle it properly and was able to stoke the fires. He had to rake the fire flat, as flat as a spirit level would show. This ensured that the fire burnt economically and produced the maximum heat. The day was a long one from six in the morning until six at night. The last job of the day for the stoker was to riddle the fire before the next watch came on duty. This meant turning big wheels at either side of the firebox and was done at the end of each shift. Bert proved to be a keen and quick learner and soon became a very good stoker.

For a period of three happy years both boys fitted in well and proved their worth. Bert's pay was the sum of two shillings a week. The captain kept back and handed out money as and when it was needed. Bert saved during those three years as the opportunity to spend did not come around too often. He made trips in and out of the port of London heading to some interesting places around the world. Amongst these trips were those from the naval base at Chatham to Gibraltar, which he still remembers as a beautiful sight.

This happy period in their life came to an end when the captain informed the crew that the shipping line of only three or four ships was being taken over by another line. The new company only wanted the ships, and this necessitated paying off of the crew in London. Bert received his well-earned money and the captain gave him a stoker's ticket as he had proved himself to be competent and reliable in his work.

At the Seaman's Mission in London the boys, now 16 and 18 years old, were allocated a bed, were fed morning and evening and provided with a sandwich and bottle of lemonade for their mid-day meal. The evening meal was kept aside for any resident who was late back to the mission due to distances involved in job searching. They were expected to look for a job and find employment as quickly as possible. Bert searched for two weeks trying at the docks to find another stoker's job on board any of the ships that used the port of London. Sadly, nothing was available.

On a whim and feeling despondent, Bert set out early one Friday morning and walked to Bermondsey, a good hour's walk away. There were many warehouses and firms there. Sadly, after a good part of the day still no job had materialised. Bert was on his way back to the mission when he spotted a sign asking for a driver and a fireman outside a firm by the name of Pickfords. In he went and saw the boss. The man looked at Bert in a questioning manner unsure of what this slight youth wanted of him. Bert said he was looking for a job. The man asked him what he thought he could do. Bert explained about his experience at sea and as a stoker he felt he could take on the job of fireman in the firm. That was the name given to the job stoking on steam engines. Bert showed him his stoker's ticket. This seemed to satisfy the man, but he was concerned when Bert told him where he was staying. However, Bert assured him he would walk to work and be on time.

On returning to the Seaman's Mission he informed them that he had found a job. Unfortunately, this meant he was given a month's notice to find other accommodation. This was a worrying time for Bert. However, sandwiches would be made for him for his lunch with the bottle of lemonade and his evening meal would be kept for him whilst still a resident at the mission.

Bert arrived in good time at ten minutes past seven after an hour's walk to begin his first day at seven thirty. He was introduced to the engine driver who appeared to Bert to be a friendly and pleasant chap. Bert had no difficulty settling in to his job. He knew how to stoke and rake the fire. This later task intrigued the engine driver. Stoked properly it also proved more efficient as the boss later discovered, less fuel was used and the power output was improved. Bert was proving his worth very quickly indeed and he receive the pay of a pound a week to begin with.

The engine driver explained to Bert that from time to time their work would take them away overnight, and when this happened they would stay in bed and board accommodation. He was told that notice would be given to him enabling him to bring a change of clothing. All was well except for this worry over new accommodation. During the first lunch break the driver found out something about his new working companion. He listened attentively as Bert told him a little bit about himself, where he was living and the need to find new lodgings.

The following day the morning progressed with a job off the site and the transportation of heavy engines. The night before Bert had dampened down the fire so all would be ready in the morning, which impressed the driver and boss. The lunch break came late at two o'clock and Bert was in for a pleasant surprise. The engine driver informed him that he and his wife had discussed

Bert's predicament and wished to offer him lodgings in their box room. Bert couldn't believe his good fortune. The room would be ready as soon as the engine driver's wife had purchased a bed and the necessary linen. The house was a small terraced house; two up and two down as Bert described it, yet very comfortable and very near to Pickfords depot. The house was situated on North Street.

Work had to take place on Saturday morning to prepare for a big job on Monday. The necessary equipment had to be got ready. On the previous day the engine driver had informed Bert that the room was ready whenever he wished to move in. Bert was quick to suggest the next day, Saturday. This proved convenient and he was invited to arrive in time for his supper at six o'clock. When asked if he had much to move Bert said he could get all his possessions neatly wrapped in a parcel bundled up in paper and tied with string. His only possession was a change of clothing.

Bert informed the warden at the Mission to Seaman that he would be vacating his room the following day as he was moving into his new lodgings. The warden asked him about his meal on Saturday as he was aware Saturday was a working day. Bert informed him he had been invited for a six o'clock supper. The warden wished Bert well and gave him a pound to start him on his new venture. At this stage in his life he could not believe his good fortune. Bert walked to work and back to the mission on the Saturday and then returned to North Street at the pre-arranged time. The engine driver's wife, according to Bert, was a typical working class Londoner. The wife of the engine driver arranged the weekly rent of twenty-five shillings and this would provide Bert with a room, meals and laundry but not much more.

Bert was observant, worked hard and learnt all that he could during that first year. His work for Pickfords Heavy Haulage took him all over the country. In many cases, overnight stays were essential and in some cases the stay lasted several days. The reason being that the company attempted to pick up work on the return journey to London, thus avoiding an unprofitable journey. Bert became familiar with not only important routes in the United Kingdom, but came to know London extremely well. This was of paramount importance when maneuvering these very big heavy haulage vehicles and their trailers, some of which were over eighty feet in length and many feet high. His assigned driver was a pleasant man whom he had digs with and who encouraged and instructed Bert in the ways of heavy haulage, lifting heavy machinery and keeping engines running under all conditions. It was a happy and secure time in his life.

At home Bert's accommodation, though modest, was comfortable and gave Bert the experience of a real home for the first time in his life. Very different from the boys home in which he had spent several years.

At the age of seventeen the time had come to approach the boss and give a clear indication of how he wished to progress within the firm. Bert was always direct in his approach, and very certain of his own capabilities. His first year had been deemed a success and one that had benefited the company. Bert had shown initiative and the ability to learn, growing skilled as a fireman. The boss asked Bert what he wanted to do and where he felt his future lay within the firm. Bert was quick to reply, he wanted to be a driver. This might appear simple and a natural progression but bearing in mind that he was just seventeen, of slight build, and the engines and vehicles were large and required a considerable amount of strength as well as skill to handle, it was something of a challenge. This did not daunt young Bert so the boss pointed to a large motor vehicle and said, "from tomorrow learn to drive and handle that vehicle".

In the firm's yard the first problem for Bert was starting the motor as there was no driving instructor or instruction. This had to be accomplished manually with a starting handle. The past year had been a learning year and good observation had shown him how this should be done. The gear lever had to be placed in reverse before attempting to start the motor. There was considerable skill involved and Bert had to develop this skill, as he did not have the strength of some men. After a considerable amount of trial and error and the cautious moving of the lever a little further up the scale to forward the motor started. Once started, the driving commenced and he found he could drive the vehicle forward and improved on the handling as the day progressed. Then came the time for reversing and this proved a very difficult task and one in which he did not resolve on that first day.

Throughout the evening and night Bert mulled over the driving problem and analysed what should be happening to the vehicle when in reverse; in particular the relationship between the steering wheel and the back of the vehicle. So on the second day as a learner driver he set out two large drums at a reasonable distance apart and with great determination started his reversing practice. The first few attempts were unsuccessful but then suddenly everything seemed to come together and from that day forward he was in complete harmony with any vehicle under his charge.

The quiet and unobtrusive observation of Bert at work happened on many occasions during his first few years with Pickfords. Bert was being observed throughout his driving practice and the boss was pleased and confident enough after observing Bert's progress to assign him as driver of one of their vehicles. The day arrived when he was given his first assignment, which was to collect a huge propeller from the docks and deliver the load to Southampton. Off he set with his assistant.

He drove slowly and safely to the docks. On arrival he discovered he would need to reverse into a fairly narrow gateway to load his cargo. This he did after a full assessment of the situation. Once loaded he set off on the first leg of the journey across London. His knowledge of London and safe routes was essential and he progressed slowly but safely and successfully to the outskirts of the city. Then came the parking of the vehicle for a well-earned lunch stop. The journey continued to Southampton without any problems and culminated in the safe delivery of his load. The return journey to London was a good clear run. Unbeknown to Bert he had been observed through this first journey. His boss had followed him all the way not so much to check on Bert, but to come to his assistance should he get into difficulty as Bert was just seventeen and the task assigned was not an easy one. Bert finished this first job with a feeling of satisfaction although extremely tired and with his body aching. This was to be expected, as in those early days of motoring there was no power assistance with brakes, steering or gear change.

On my asking Bert about using the assistance of the police when on a journey either in London or further afield, he had a definite opinion, and one he had made at a tender age. He recounted the time he and his assistant were hauling a particularly wide and high load across London. Bert knew the route well and on this occasion he had a police escort. All went well until they reached Putney Bridge. The police escort continued straight ahead and did not turn to proceed across the bridge. Bert stopped and waited. The escort returned with a puzzled look expecting Bert to say there was a mechanical problem, but no, Bert explained he was not taking that route but would turn across Putney bridge. An argument ensued, but Bert stood firm. He would not budge. The police escort contacted the station, the station insisted the prescribed route was the one to take but Bert stood firm. This is good evidence of Bert's clear thinking and determination, even as a very young man. Finally, after a thorough check by the police, they had to concede that Bert was right in his assessment of the situation and he would not have been able to take his vehicle on such a route as there was a low arch, too low for his load. So across Putney Bridge the convoy proceeded with a sheepish apology from the police. Bert was always cautious about involving the police. He preferred to rely on his own knowledge and skill and most importantly his own assessment of the situation.

Pickfords moved from Bermondsey to another London site and Bert continued for a further fifty happy and rewarding years becoming one of the company's foremost and most experienced drivers. He had learned all he had to about the petrol engine whilst making the transition from steam.

Bert retired from the firm at the age of sixty-six, a year beyond the normal retirement age. He was delighted to have received a golden handshake of £1000 as a token of his loyalty and dedication to the firm. Bert continued to work for another nineteen years, it was three years after that that he told me this story, and he was still going out to a local café when being visited by a very attractive young woman not half his age.

Gerald Chegwidden

THE TREASURER'S CHALLENGE – 2018

<u>GREAT LAKES HERE WE COME</u>

John's retirement challenge was to sail his boat to the great lakes of North America! So in 1986 he supervised the building of Caramor (Celtic 'for love of the sea') a Rustler 36, at the Penryn Yard, with a full keel-stepped mast, and a larger rudder for the 'larger seas'. The next few years, until May 1991, were spent getting to know Caramor and gaining plenty of sailing experience, crossing Biscay, going around the U.K., PLUS Holland and the Channel Islands.

The first leg of our journey would be to cross the Atlantic to the Caribbean in mid-November, in order to avoid 'the hurricane season' in the summer, leaving from the Canary Islands. We said our goodbyes to family and friends on May 1st 1991 from Falmouth, but only sailed across to St. Mawes as there a full scale gale blowing in Biscay. Our crew consisted of John's sister Anne and ourselves.

For the next ten weeks we day sailed in the Mediterranean, we visited Spain, Portugal, Gibraltar and Perpignan in France. In early September, back in Gibraltar, Caramor was lifted out of the water for pressure hosing and to have the hull anti-fouled. We re-vitalled the boat with both dry and fresh goods and John and I both had our hair cut very short! John's son Chris flew in to join us for the next leg of the journey.

In mid-September we departed The Rock and gradually acclimatized to the Atlantic roll as we sailed to Porto Santo and Madeira. It was between these islands that John's main fear was realised with a whale swimming alongside us. We put the engine on immediately so there was no misunderstanding that we may be a fellow whale and, thankfully, he didn't dive underneath the boat. After spending two weeks exploring Madeira we continued our cruise to the Canary Islands, ending in Tenerife. Here we had a change of crew. Chris returned to the U.K. and our sailing friend John joined us for the 'Big Crossing.'

Caramor was re-vitalled with fresh meat, fruit and vegetables (green wherever possible), as well as plenty of bottled water. Leaving Puerto Colon marina on November 13th, which was not a Friday, we set sail in a south-westerly direction. After a couple of days, we picked up the Trade Winds and it took us to Barbados. The seas were big and it took a few days for stomachs to get used to the swell, despite having been on board for many months already. We each stood rolling three hour watches throughout the night and during the day. Where possible John recommended that we built up our sleep reserve, in case of an emergency.

We ate well on board with roasts, stews, Cornish pasties (of course) mincemeat tarts, freshly baked bread and not to be forgotten, Anne's egg and cress sandwiches. The cress was actually sown and tended on board. When all the fresh food had been eaten we had to be more innovative with our tinned supplies. At times we trailed a fishing line and, on one occasion, we caught a Dorado, which is a fish of the tuna family. This was duly sedated in the cockpit by pouring brandy into its gills, which was a tip passed onto us earlier in the trip. It provided a couple of very welcome fresh meals.

Dolphins often swam with the boat, leaping in the bow wave and we also had a display of hump back whales from afar. We regularly had flying fish on the deck in the morning, but these were, sadly, too small to eat. We sighted Shearwaters, Skuas, Storm Petrels, Gannets and Roseate Terns.

John loved the navigation part of the trip and used his sextant regularly to take our position from the sun. Another crew member, also named John, was good at star and galaxy recognition. He shared his knowledge with us when the night skies were amazingly clear. Our only special electronic gadget on board was our emergency satellite beacon, which we fortunately didn't need to activate.

We only passed a couple of merchant ships and one cruise liner on our Atlantic crossing and happily there were no serious storms. On the evening of December 2nd 1991 we sighted lights on the horizon and by midnight we had dropped anchor in Carlisle Bay, Barbados. It had taken us 19 days to travel 2,737 nautical miles. After celebrating with a glass of bubbly, we toasted the Skipper and 'turned in', well pleased with our achievement.

During the next couple of months, we cruised many of the Caribbean islands, visited The Bahamas and crossed the Gulf Stream to West Palm Beach in Florida. From there we made our way north to New York via the Intra Coastal Waterway which runs parallel to the Atlantic Ocean. The further north we sailed the colder the weather became and in mid-March in North Carolina it began to snow. We were so cold that we decided to backtrack and head south!

Now we were ready to continue to Norfolk V. A. and the 'Big Apple.' We recorded our arrival in the city with a photo of Caramor and her crew by the Statue of Liberty.

We were at last ready to enter the final stage of our journey to the Great Lakes, sailing up The Hudson river. With the mast lowered on the deck we made our way through a system of locks and canals and the Mohawk River to reach our destination. We finally entered Lake Ontario, had the mast re-stepped, and began our exploration of the lakes.

Not a bad way to mark a retirement!

John and Cynthia Dowding.

THE TREASURER'S CHALLENGE – 2018

LIGHTS, CAMERA, SAT NAV!

Since Qualifying to be an A.D.I (Approved Driving Instructor) back in December 2003, I have always valued my situation of being Self Employed and having control to a certain extent over my working life.

Even though I was Self-employed, I started working with a well-established Driving School covering the Truro/Falmouth Area. I remember my first customer. I had done the training and got my brand new certificate displayed in the car, which allowed me to teach for professional payment, but just because someone is a good driver, it doesn't necessarily mean he would be good at teaching it to someone. I had to live up to the status that well-earned certificate gave me. It was not just a case of getting my customers through their tests, but making sure they were at a suitable level to be safe on our modern roads.

I met my first customer. She was very pleasant. I didn't let on that it was my first person I was teaching since qualifying. The lesson went well and over the coming weeks I built up a good base of customers.

As it turned out, that person who was my first customer, was my first customer to pass both the theory and practical tests. I was there at the test centre at Camborne. Her nervousness was understandable nervous, but I didn't let on that privately I was nervous also, as at this point my pass count was zero and I wanted my novice to get me a pass on the board.

Well, I seem to remember that three candidates went out on their tests at that time. As the other two returned and their instructors went to meet them, I became aware that they had both failed, or as it is commonly stated, "been unsuccessful on this occasion." We haven't quite got to the stage of using the politically correct statement of "Deferred Success". They left, and I wondered where my car was. Then it came into sight, and back into the test centre it came. It was a pass!!!!!!

Naturally my candidate was delighted. I was over the moon for my newly qualified driver and privately delighted as I had my first test pass on the board. I'm very glad I didn't do what I felt like doing, which was a lap of honour around the test centre.

I was with that Driving School for nearly two and a half years before I went independent in June 2006.

Many times I have waited for my candidates to return from their tests which last around 35 – 40 minutes. In the earlier days when I was still using my first Corsa, which had hub caps on the wheels, I saw my car come back through the gate with its front left hub cap missing. I don't know why, but I didn't feel the chances that they had passed were very good. Indeed, I was told they had committed a serious steering fault. The examiner said to me "If you want your hub cap back, it's in Drump Road, a couple of miles back in Redruth."

That was a thankfully rare occurrence. There have been many different celebrations of results over the years. It's not uncommon when people have passed their tests to phone others to inform them of the good news before we leave the test centre. There was a time someone informed their workmates and I heard down the speakerphone "They have passed ", followed by a huge cheer.

There was also an occasion when we had been asked to phone the shop where the person worked to tell the owner if they had passed or failed. My opening words to the person on the other end of the line were, "Do you sell driving test congratulations cards?" They soon realized it was good news and I have been told they then ran around the shop fridges in celebration!

We have to be very careful to explain to a learner exactly what we want them to do. I once asked someone who hadn't had many lessons at that stage, to turn on the lights while we were driving along. They went to change a control and I looked to see the light symbol had come up on the dash board. I became concerned that the whole dash board had gone out completely! They had actually turned the engine off. I didn't panic. I calmly asked them to restart the car and told them where the switch to the lights as.

People often say I'm brave to do what I do. Well, it does have its risks, but at the end of the day, I actually don't worry too much about teaching my learners, as I have Dual Controls and will only put them in a situation when I feel they are ready to deal with it. I can think of many jobs where people have to be brave. Where I do feel more concerned, is with the actions of other drivers. Most are fine, some very polite and helpful, but some are unbelievable.

Just recently, my learner was making good progress on a hill going along a main road. A couple of cars overtook us, then another driver thought he could get by us even though arrows are telling him to not overtake. He then overtook us showering us with grit from the middle of the road and we saw him again a couple of cars ahead stopped at the roundabout. Was it really worth it my friend?

Change is always a part of life and in 2010 the new part of the driving test which required the candidate to follow road signs for part of the test instead of fully being given directions was introduced. This was a good dynamic to bring into the test, as people are not going to always have someone sitting next to them giving directions. Not long after this change came in, I was being informed by an examiner who has since retired, that my candidate had missed a couple of signs, to which I said in an effort to make a valid point with a bit of humour, "well some of the signs are quite dodgy" I was then told "well they're not if you look at them." So I felt put in my place and realised humour was not always going to be appreciated in these situations. That particular examiner passed many of my candidates over the years, so it wasn't held against me.

I also remarked once when told that someone had failed, that the person "didn't normally make that mistake." I was swiftly reminded that "they can only mark what they see on the day", which is perfectly true of course.

I often get asked about things people hear regarding test results. I tell people my honest feeling. If someone's driving is good enough, they will pass. It's a waste of time speculating over nonsense about what day or time it is, etc.

Another change came to the test in December 2017, Candidates are no longer tested on Turn in the Road (commonly known as the three-point turn) or reverse around a corner. We are still advised to teach these exercises. In has come reversing on the right, and now going into actual car parks and parking forward in a bay. The reverse into a bay and parallel park exercises still remain as options. The examiner asks candidates to carry out one of these procedures and may in addition require them to perform an emergency stop.

As reported in the press there is now a Sat Nav element to most tests. It requires the candidate to follow instructions from the Sat Nav for around half the test. Some people are asked to follow the road signs instead.

After approaching 15 years doing this job, I can say I feel privileged and proud to have helped so many people achieve their goal and get their full licence. I feel great delight when someone passes their test, and still feel like the world has ended if they fail.

I never believed when I started that here in 2018 I would be teaching people with a sat nav and, of course, I now have cameras in my car on the front and rear. We can review any situation that has occurred and of course

I can record and play back the visual footage of the driving tests.

I hope to continue doing this for a while yet. It's been a great positive in my life.   David Simmons.

THE TREASURER'S CHALLENGE – 2018

CLOSE ENCOUNTERS OF A MEDICAL KIND

I was fortunate to train in London and was taught in the traditional style, which as now I look back over 40 years, I view as a great privilege.

I had only been to London twice in my life and was looked upon by my fellow students as a country bumpkin! The majority of our intake were from wealthy backgrounds and had gone to some of the most famous public schools. Most were single sex schools, whereas I had attended a co-education grammar school. I had grown up with the wonder of the female sex but for most of my friends, girls were a new discovery, but they became fast learners.

In addition to the medical school at Westminster there was a school of nursing. In London each medical school had a similar set up and each hospital had its own individual nurses' uniform. I always felt our nurses looked the best. The uniform was a pale blue with a crisp white apron, detachable collar, short sleeves and white cuffs. A fob watch was pinned on the apron and our nurses wore black stockings!

Student nurses wore plain white hats and, when qualified, these changed to what were known as 'frillies'. A name which denoted other items of clothing!

Training in the same hospital was great and there was a real sense of family. In those days there was a nurses' sick bay and our nurses were always looked after by the most senior physicians and surgeons. The Nurse Sick Bay was strictly out of bounds and patrolled by a large, busty, Hattie Jaques style of matron.

On one occasion Freda, a friend, was admitted with an appendicitis. Concerned about her recovery, my two flatmates planned a secret visit to boost her recovery. Having crept past the guards they found her room and were cheering her up when they heard the patter of huge footsteps. In trepidation, they hid in the wardrobe.

Peering through the gap they watched the matronly figure standing sideways like a galleon in full sail. They found it impossible to stop giggling and eventually fell out of the wardrobe exclaiming "it's a fair cop Guv!" They were then ejected.

In the same way the nurses home situated on the Vauxhall Bridge Road was out of bounds, its entrance patrolled by a uniformed guard complete with hat. He sat at a desk in one of those old mahogany swivel chairs, reading the Daily Mirror behind a counter with a hinged top that lifted up like a pub bar. It must have looked amusing as three tall lads crept behind each other like a pantomime caterpillar over the Wilton carpet of the foyer to be greeted by the amused doorman who exclaimed "why don't you walk through the door like everyone else?" I guess he was adjusting to the morals of the seventies!

As students we would experience the emergency admissions and be allocated on call rooms which were at the 5th floor of the medical school. The room was equipped with a single bed and a white porcelain wall-hung sink. The nearest toilet was in the basement. Our female students would share similar facilities. One rather naïve friend, Sarah, asked "what do we do if we need to have a pee at night?" and in true medical student fashion the reply came, "use the sink of course!"

All was fine until the next night on call when Sarah needed to answer the call of nature and used the sink. One's knowledge of anatomy will confirm it was not so easy for her, and the result was that the sink was displaced from its brackets and the room flooded by the fractured cold water pipe!

On another occasion my flat-mate Roy decided to use an on call duty room as a bolt after a rather inebriated session in one of the many burgeoning clubs in the city. This saved a trip back to our flat in Battersea. In his drunken state he took off all his clothes and collapsed in a heap on the single bed. In the early hours of the morning he needed to answer the call of nature and on this occasion decided to get the lift down to the basement. Standing, half asleep the cold white porcelain of the urinal sent a shiver through his body and he realised he was standing completely naked. The only way back was via the lift to the fifth floor and it always stopped at ground floor level. The doors opened revealing Roy standing starkers and our experienced night porter simply said, "Goodnight, Mr. Isworth!"

We were privileged to be taught by some eminent medical consultants. As students we were identified by wearing short white coats. Groups of about 6 were attached to what was described as a firm. We would travel around the wards following the eminent men who may have visiting specialists from abroad, Senior Registrars, Registrars, Senior Housemen, Housemen and us, the humble students. As the entourage passed through the hospital my friend Guy, who always said what he felt, started to sing 'there's no business like show business.' He was later severely ticked off by the Dean.

On one occasion, standing at the foot of the bed, we were shown a sample of urine from a man newly diagnosed with diabetes. We were shown his boots and observed the traces of white sugar crystals on the top where, over time, his sugary urine had crystallised on the leather. The consultant opened the urine sample and dipped his finger in it. He then sealed the silver lid and licked a finger.

"I want you to repeat what I have done, and tell me what you noticed."

We all dipped a digit and proudly exclaimed, "it tastes sweet, Sir."

"That is true," was his reply. He then, with a wry smile, explained that "medicine and diagnosis are all about observation. If you noticed I dipped my index finger into the urine, but actually licked my middle finger!"

Our consultants were distinguished, elegant and appeared imposing to a first year student. Many wore London tailored Savile Row suits and shirts with detachable collars and cuffs sporting a variety of cufflinks. They spoke with an air of authority, with accents I later heard on 'Brideshead Revisited.' There was a clear distinction between the physicians and surgeons; the latter being much more harsh in their words if one dared to get an answer wrong. I remember one retort after making a mistake.

"Rogers, I am going to throw you away like a used condom!"

But one had huge respect for those who possessed such a high level of technical skill, compassion and humanity.

In those days our specialists could be called to the homes of wealthy people who were happy to pay their fee always in guineas. On one occasion a physician was called to an important household where the elderly mother was in a severe costive state! He attended with his Senior Registrar. Having examined the lady carefully he asked if he could have a silver teaspoon to help relieve the difficult impaction. A liveried butler arrived with a silver teaspoon covered by a napkin on a silver tray. The specialist relieved the problem, washed the spoon, and put it in the top pocket of his immaculate Savile Row suit. In the taxi back to the hospital the concerned Registrar enquired whether his boss was in the habit of stealing silver from the privileged household. The reply was, "No, but I occasionally take tea there!"

On another occasion an eminent Gynaecologist was summoned to a private household and needed to perform an intimate examination. In a hospital setting it is much easier to perform this check on a proper couch. It is much more tricky when faced with a soft flock mattress which dipped in the middle. During the check he found, to his embarrassment, that his silk tie had become stuck in an awkward position. With great panache his Registrar deftly produced a pair of scissors and cut the tie in half. From then on the specialist practiced his medicine wearing a silk bow tie.

After several years, much study and the rigours of one's finals, my attention was focused on which branch of medicine to follow. I was asked to apply for the Professor of Medicine's firm, which was a great accolade, but I had decided to follow a career as a GP. I soon realised that I needed to experience as much acute medicine as possible and my first House job was at Queen Mary's Hospital, Roehampton. This was a busy hospital and provided a huge variety of acute cases.

My heart was calling me home to Cornwall and as I moved west, my next job was House Surgeon at Winchester. Here I experienced a great variety of acute surgery. The job was fascinating and I learned to work very long hours, to be on call for 24 hours day and night for a week, with only one afternoon free.

In the late seventies, joining General Practice was a favourite career choice and I was one of the two successful applicants out of 48 to be enrolled on the new GP training scheme based at Treliske. One of the posts was in St. Mawes and this had married accommodation. The other post was in Redruth. I was unmarried then and was assigned to Green Lane Surgery, Redruth. Prior to starting my year as trainee, I worked for two years in a variety of hospital posts, reinforcing my knowledge of the wide range of specialities I would need as a GP.

During this time, I met Lorraine, who had taken a temporary job as Night Sister at West Cornwall Hospital, prior to her joining the QE2. As a result of a chance meeting helping me suture a patient, she lost the opportunity of travelling as an experienced nurse on a luxury liner, visiting exotic places, to become a GP's wife, partner and soul mate in Redruth.

I greatly admired her skill, compassion and total commitment to her profession. She had started as a cadet nurse at 15, and for me, has always been the ultimate nurse. I appreciate that as we get older we look back and make comments such as "in our day things were done in a proper fashion." For me, this is true, and she presented the high standards of true nursing that I value so much.

I am aware how difficult it is to cram so much of one's life and passion into a short piece of writing and am aware that I ramble on.

I must, however, mention a few stories from so many I have during my time in my beloved Redruth. One of my partners cynically commented "Redruth is Cornwall's example of life after death." For me, it was a privilege to practice for almost 40 years in one of the last true Cornish towns, where there is still a sense of family commitment. It is strange when I visit the town to remember with vivid detail many of the houses I visited, as if there is a video recorder playing in my head.

There were so many funny stories.

In the later part of my time, the demand from our patients grew and we introduced a triage system, where patients could speak to the duty doctor by telephone. I remember one old lady ringing up complaining of a pain between her breasts. I enquired whether the pain was across her upper chest and she replied, "no dear, these days it is more in the upper abdomen!"

On another occasion, I was sitting in my consultation room, which was room 4, and the receptionist called into the waiting room, "Mrs. Williams, room 4" In walked a little old lady, wearing a buttoned up gabardine mac, followed by an old man, who sat behind her. She explained she had bronchitis. I asked her to slip off her blouse, examined her chest, and she then dressed. I prescribed some medication and she thanked me and left. The old man remained seated and I enquired whether he wanted to ask me anything about his wife. He replied, "That's not my wife. The receptionist said Mr. Williams room 4!" Neither had said anything during my examination!

I have often thought my vocation as a GP was similar to a parish priest. It was a privilege to be allowed into people's lives; to experience the frailties and strength of people which makes one appreciate one's own strength and weakness; to share their joy and to deeply feel the pain of loss and sadness. It was difficult to try to learn to leave much of the emotion at work and not bring it home. I was once asked what did I learn and I commented that men are different to women!

I also learned that the most important value in bringing up children was to give them love and I witnessed this is in some of the poorest families. Also, I learned to understand and accept people who are angry and aggressive, the importance of listening and sharing one's own life experience. Most of all, I found out that acts of kindness go a long way in this world and it is best never to judge and to treat everyone the same. I guess all this rambling thought comes back to Christ's teaching and I hope our country returns to his message.

One final story. One of my patients was a wonderfully kind man with a deep Cornish voice. He worked as a greengrocer and would supply some of the outlying villages with fruit and vegetables from his travelling van. He lived in a small council house which was sparsely furnished. On the cream tiled mantelpiece was a small plaster model of a figure with writing. It was simply painted with the text "I complained I had no shoes until I met a man who had no feet." He told me he would rush around the country and often see an old man leaning on a five bar gate, looking into the distance towards Falmouth. One day he stopped and said to the man, "I often watch you looking into the distance. Don't you wish you were there?"

THE TREASURER'S CHALLENGE – 2018

He replied, "what's there that isn't here?"

Tim Rogers.

<u>THE FUNERAL</u>

Shafts of sunlight through the glass,
soft organ music from the past.
Loving and peaceful is the scene,
someone's coming home at last.

Pain and sorrow have no place,
the mood is good, there is no rush,
All is tranquil, calm and chaste,
laid to rest, and free from haste.

Thoughtful friends recount the past,
the struggles of an early life,
The ups and downs that went so fast,
now free from pain, and earthly strife.

This loving scene is filled with joy,
serene quiet happiness, and love
from all those touched by this short life,
A grateful thanks to him above.

Alan Arthur Rawlinson

THE TREASURER'S CHALLENGE – 2018

CUSGARNE, MARCH 2018

Snow is drifting, long and hard.
Thoughts are pulsing fast
Beauty of the garden white, covered by such mystic light.
Happy thoughts around me flow
Full of laughter, full of fun.

Snow is falling in Cusgarne
Beauty from our God above
Teaching all that it is love
That keeps each mortal well aware
To honour life and never care
That material goods cannot compare.

It's snowflakes falling from the sky
A sign to all that God is nigh.

CEDAR OF LEBANON

Cedar of Lebanon
Streams of time spill
Through your quiet fingers.
Your open hands are a place to rest in
Your immobility is the rhythm of your stillness.
Cedar of Lebanon, so removed, so calm.

Gill Farnworth

THE TREASURER'S CHALLENGE – 2018

<u>ON BEING WITH THE BELOVED</u>

I look before me.
The brilliant whiteness of Los Olivios dazzles,
Nestled in an oasis of olive trees.
Their dark green leaves so different from the
neighbouring almonds.

I look down.
The village passed moments ago is miniscule.
The unmade track winds up the mountain, clinging
precariously to the side.
I remember my heart beating rapidly riding in the taxi,
Aware of the steep drop, centimetres from my side.

I look up.
A lone tree is silhouetted against the azure sky.
The steep mountains surround, their pathways
beckoning to be conquered.
The snow still tops the Sierra Nevada peeping out
between,
Even though it is now June.

I look around.
The grasses sway in the wind when I turn from the
shelter of the wall.
A myriad of colour lies at my feet as wildflowers bloom in
profusion.
And I marvel
At God's creation.

Chris Ryall – Written after a retreat in Spain, June 2018

THE TREASURER'S CHALLENGE – 2018

THE MAGIC BOX

I will put into the box
The swish of a shooting star at night
Fire from a tiger's eye
Rainbow colours of a butterfly.

Snowy sugar taste of sweets
The hottest sun of holidays in France
The dancing ballerina on stage.

My box is finished from ice and God's .....
With roses that smell sweet on the lid
With fairy wings on the corners
And shimmering gold birds flying in the hinges
With white sun rising at midnight.

Rowan Searle (Aged 6)

HAIKU – BEARDED DRAGON

Scales are shining
The eating of the locust
Puffing of the beard

Oliver Searle (Aged 9)

THE TREASURER'S CHALLENGE – 2018

<u>MY GRANDMOTHER'S POEM</u>

Beautiful faces are they that wear
The light of a pleasant spirit there;
Beautiful hands are they that do
The deeds that are noble, good and true;
Beautiful feet are they that go
Simply to lighten another's woe.

Written by my Grandmother, E. Marie Cleave on
November 29th 1903. Contributed by Barbara Wood.

THE TREASURER'S CHALLENGE – 2018

ST. PIRAN

Would I have liked to meet him, do you think?
That man – not old then surely, but strong and vigorous,
Staggering, salt-stained from his amazing craft
Shaped like a millstone (A coracle, perhaps?)

Would I have watched and whispered while he built
(Or found) himself a prayer-cell on the hill,
And looked on, astounded, with the rest
When he found water in a ferny dell –
So pure and crystal, in those germ-filled days
It soothed and cleansed old suppurating sores,
Brought cool relief to parched and fevered lips?

And when that radical, strange tale
That fuelled his faith, what would have happened then?
Would I have been inspired, or appalled?
Would I have turned away in disbelief
Preferring the old gods of stream and stone?
Or might I have been brave enough to dare
And grasp the new –
The bright white cross of hope against the dark,
That flutters still
Atop flagstaffs of this ancient land?

Rosemary Aitken

THE TREASURER'S CHALLENGE – 2018

When I was at College studying to be a teacher, we were confronted one day by the following and asked what we could make of them. See how you get on.

Paul Stuart

THE COSMOLOGICAL ARGUMENT

"If there is nothing eternal, then there can be no becoming: for there must be something which undergoes the process of becoming, that is, that from which things come to be; and the last member of this series must be ungenerated, for the series must start with something, since nothing can come from nothing." Aristotle, "Metaphysics."

"The existence of God can be proved in five ways.

The first is the argument from motion. It is certain, and evident to our senses, that in the world some things are in motion. Now, whatever is moved is moved by another, for nothing can be moved except it is in potentiality to that towards it is moved; whereas a thing moves in as much as it is in act. For motion is nothing else than the reduction of something from potentiality to actuality. But nothing can be reduced from potentiality to actuality, except by something in a state of actuality. Thus, that which is actually hot, as fire, makes wood, which is potentially hot, to be actually hot, and thereby moves and changes it. Now, it is not possible that the same thing should be at once in actuality and potentiality in the same respect, but only in different respects. For what is actually hot cannot simultaneously be potentially hot; but it is simultaneously potentially cold. It is therefore impossible that in the same respect and in the same way a thing should be both mover and moved. That is, it should move itself. Therefore, whatever is moved must be moved by another. If that by which it is moved be itself moved, then this also must needs be moved by another, and that by another again. But this cannot go on to infinity, because then there would be no first mover, and, consequently, no other mover, seeing that subsequent movers move only in as much as they are moved by the first mover; as the staff moves only because it is moved by the hand. Therefore, it is necessary to arrive at a first mover, moved by no other; and this understands to be God.

The second way is from the nature of efficient cause. In the world of sensible things, we find that there is an order of efficient causes. There is no case in which a thing is to be the efficient cause of itself; for so it would be prior to itself, which is impossible. Now, in efficient causes it is not possible to go on to infinity, because in all efficient causes following in order, the first is the cause of the intermediate cause, and the intermediate cause is the cause of the ultimate cause, whether the intermediate cause be several, or one only. Now, to take away the cause is to take away the effect. Therefore, if there be no first cause among efficient causes, there will be no ultimate, nor any intermediate, cause. But if in efficient causes it is possible to go on to infinity, there will be no first cause efficient cause, neither will there be an ultimate effect, nor any intermediate efficient causes; all of which is plainly false. Therefore, it is necessary to admit a first efficient cause, to which everyone gives the name of God."

St. Thomas Aquinas, "Summa Theologica."

THE ONTOLOGICAL ARGUMENT

"And so, O Lord, since thou givest understanding to faith, give me to understand that thou dost exist, as we believe, and that thou art what we believe thee to be. Now we believe that thou art a being than which nothing greater can be thought. Or can it be that there is no such being, since "the fool hath said in his heart, there is no God"? (Psalm 14 v. 1) But **when** this same fool hears what I am saying – "a being than which none greater can be thought" -he understands what he hears, and what he understands is in his understanding, even if he does not understand that it exists. For it is one thing for an object to be in the understanding, and another thing to understand that it exists. When a painter considers beforehand what he is going to paint, he has it in his understanding, but he does not suppose that what he has in his understanding, but he does not suppose that what he has not yet painted already exists. But when he has painted it, he both has it in his understanding and understands that what he has now produced exists. Even the fool, then, must be convinced that a being than which none greater can be thought exists at least in his understanding, since when he hears this he understands it, and whatever is understood is in the understanding. But clearly that than which a greater cannot be thought cannot exist in the understanding alone. For if it is actually in the understanding alone, it can be thought of as existing also in reality, and this is greater. Therefore, if that than which a greater cannot be thought is in the understanding alone, this same thing than which a greater cannot be thought is that than which a greater can be thought. But, obviously, this is impossible. Without doubt, therefore, there exists, both in the understanding and in reality, something than which a greater cannot be thought.

And certainly it exists so truly that it cannot be thought of as non-existent. For something can be thought of as existing, which cannot be thought of as not existing, and this is greater than that which can be thought of as not existing. Thus, if that than which a greater cannot be thought can be thought of as not existing, this very thing than which a greater cannot be thought is not that which a greater cannot be thought. But this is contradictory. So, then, there truly is a being than which a greater cannot be thought – so truly that it cannot even be thought of as not existing.

And thou art this being, O Lord our God."

St. Anselm. (1033-1109)

THE TREASURER'S CHALLENGE – 2018

RIDDLES

Q: I skip and zoom across the pond. I have two wings. What am I?
A: A dragonfly.

Bethan (Aged 7)

Q: I am never thirsty, but I am always drinking. What am I?
A: A fish

Q: It's a place to go but when you're in it, you're nowhere. What am I?
A: A black hole

Rowan Searle (Aged 9)

PRACTICE WRITINGS

This is a practice piece for a creative writing group, U3A- 2004 and is a paragraph written entirely with words not containing the letter 'e'. Not as easy as you might think.

Many of you know that a morning in your pyjamas is a day that starts in a good way. Wrong! Rising at dawn on a crisp morning and going out into bright sunlight, crossing a frosty lawn, crackling and sparkling in sun and shadow is such a joy, and watching a flight of birds crossing a pink dawn sky is a sight worth bottling!

So, put away your pyjamas you sluggards, go out and drink in this wondrous natural tonic that is on your lawn. It won't cost you anything. Do it daily and I'll warrant that you won't miss your laggardly ways for long. Truly, you won't!

Gill Warden

THE TREASURER'S CHALLENGE – 2018

EXAM ANSWERS

These are not made up. Students, aged 15 and 16 years, actually wrote these answers in exams!

1/. Geography:
Q: Name the 4 seasons.
A: Salt, pepper mustard and vinegar

Q: Explain one of the processes by which water can be made safe to drink.
A: Flirtation makes water safe to drink because it removes large pollutants like grit, sand, dead sheep and canoeists.

Q: How is dew formed?
A: The sun shines down on the leaves and makes them perspire.

Q: What is a planet?
A: A body of earth surrounded by sky.

Q: What causes the tides in the oceans?
A: The tides are in a fight between the Earth and the Moon. All water tends to flow towards the moon, because there is no water on the moon, and nature abhors a vacuum. I forget where the sun joins in this fight.

2/. Sociology:
Q: What guarantees may a mortgage company insist on?
A: If you are buying a house, they will insist you are well endowed.

Q: In a democratic society, how important are elections?

THE TREASURER'S CHALLENGE – 2018

A: Very important. Sex can only happen when a male gets an election.

Q: What are steroids?
A: Things for keeping carpets still on the stairs.

Q: What do you understand by the term 'free press?'
A: It's when your mother does your ironing for nothing.

Biology:
Q: What happens to your body as you age?
A: When you get old, so do your bowels and you get intercontinental.

Q: What happens to a boy when he reaches puberty?
A: He says goodbye to his boyhood and looks forward to his adultery.

Q: How can you delay milk turning sour?
A: Keep it in the cow.

Q: How are the main parts of the body categorized?
A: The body is consisted into three parts – the brainium, the   borax and the abdominal cavity. The branium contains the brain,   the   borax   contains   the heart and lungs, and the abdominal cavity contains the five bowels: A,E,I,O and U.

Q: What is the Fibula?
A: A small lie.

Q: What does "varicose" mean?
A: Nearby.

Q: Give the meaning of the term "Caesarean Section."
A: It is a district in Rome.

THE TREASURER'S CHALLENGE – 2018

Q: What is a seizure?
A: A roman emperor.

Q: What is a terminal illness?
A: When you are sick at an airport.

Q: Complete the sentence: The first cells were probably....
A: Lonely

English:
Q: Use the word "judicious" in a sentence to show you understand its meaning.
A: Hand that judicious can be soft as your face.

Q: What does the word "benign" mean?
A: Benign is what you will be after you are eight.

History:
Q: Name a person who has sailed around the world.
A: Sir Francis Drake circumcised the world.

Q: What ended in 1896?
A: 1895

Q: Where was the Magna Carta signed?
A: At the bottom

Science:
Q: Why might living next to a mobile phone be harmful to your health.
A: You could walk into it.

Q: Briefly explain what hard water is.
A: Ice

THE TREASURER'S CHALLENGE – 2018

Q: Some atoms share electrons and become more stable. Describe a situation in which people share something and everyone benefits.
A: Communism

Q: A student could not see anything when he looked down his microscope. Suggests a reason for this.
A: He is blind.

Q: Name six animals that live specifically in the Arctic.
A: Two polar bears and four seals.

Q: What are vibrations?
A: There are good vibrations and bad vibrations. Good vibrations were discovered in the 1960s.

Q: Give a reason why people might want to love near electricity pylons.
A: They could get their electricity faster than everyone else.

Religious Education:
Q: What did you think of the sermon in Assembly this morning? Give your reasoning.
A: If I had only 1 hour to live, I'd spend it listening to that sermon. It took an eternity.

THE TREASURER'S CHALLENGE – 2018

<u>STAFF DEVELOPMENT</u>

In the not too dim and distant past, people left school or University or whatever, and went into a field of endeavour or employment that they expected would last for the rest of their working lives. They gradually grew more useful as they climbed the slippery career pole upwards to the stars and a well-earned retirement.

That is not so true these days. People flit from employment pillar to employment post and a meaningful "career path" seems to have become history. One of the consequences of this unexpected job mobility is that employers haven't got as much time to devote to training and moulding their staff into useful and productive workers. For their part, new employees are expected to "hit the ground running," "think outside the box" and indulge in "blue sky" thinking. They must also pick up useful experiences along the way. Training, whether "on the job" or otherwise, is becoming an expensive luxury.

"He/she will be okay in a few days, don't worry. It's not difficult. I picked it up in less than a day!" Good management technique that. In the case of 'call handlers' there is always the all-embracing script to be used ad nauseam, and on no account must there be any attempt to answer queries that are not covered therein. That doesn't take much training, does it?

Given this dearth of meaningful staff development, I have compiled an all-embracing programme, which should help both sides of the divide. It will stand employees in good stead and provided employers with all they need to make their people blossom and actually become useful. You may be able to add to it.

Indeed, if we all sat down and gave it some serious thought, we could come up with the definitive Staff Development Programme and thus save everybody much time, effort and expense and make oodles of money in the process.

THE TREASURER'S CHALLENGE – 2018

MY DRAFT STAFF DEVELOPMENT PROGRAMME:

Self Improvement:

SE 100   Creative Suffering.
SE 101   Overcoming Peace of Mind
SE 102   Dealing with Post Realisation Depression
SE 103   Overcoming Self Doubt through Pretence and Ostentation
SE 104   Whine Your Way to Alienation
SE 105   Feigning Knowledge – A Career Advancement Strategy.
SE 106   Children – An Avoidable Distraction in Educational Decision Making. (Adapt as necessary to suit your circumstances and job).
SE 107   Keeping Facts out of the Management Structure
SE 108   Carrying a Piece of Paper While Walking Briskly

Business and Career
BC 100   The Underachievers Guide to Very Small Business Opportunities
BC 101   How to Profit From....(Fill in as required)

Fitness and Health
FH 100   Snap out of it
FH 101   Pull Yourself Together
FH 102   The Joys of Hypochondria

Home Economics and Crafts
HEC   100 Cultivating Viruses in the household or office refrigerator.
HEC   101 Needlecraft for vaccinators
HEC   102 Origami for Self-Defence (Black Belt Level course)

If all else fails, the worker, at whatever level of employment, can always fall back on an age old ruse. Get yourself a clipboard, with a pen, and move around all day looking important. If you can also appear thoughtful or to be wrestling with an intractable problem, it reinforces your status. You must occasionally stop your wandering and actually write something down, though. It doesn't matter what as nobody is ever going to look at it. Oh, if anybody challenges you, just say "can't stop; I've got to get this done before I go home. Put it in writing for me will you?"

Paul Stuart

THE TREASURER'S CHALLENGE – 2018

BLONDE AT THE PEARLY GATES

An attractive blonde lady was sent on her way to Heaven. Upon arrival, a concerned St. Peter met her the Pearly Gates.

"I'm sorry," he said, "but Heaven is suffering from an overload of Godly souls and we have something of an accommodation crisis. It has meant that we are using an entrance exam."

"That's cool," replied the woman, totally unflustered by the strange situation. "What does the exam consist of?"

"Just three questions," said St. Peter.

"No problem," she replied, "let's get on with it. I'm keen to get in."

"The first question," St. Peter said, impressed by her positive attitude, "is which two days of the week start with the letter 'T'? The second is how many seconds are there in a year and the third is what is the name of the swagman in Waltzing Matilda?"

The woman made no reaction, except to move slightly away from St. Peter, so that she didn't feel under pressure.

"I'll be back in the morning," she said.

Overnight, she gave the questions some considerable thought and you might like to do the same. She returned early the next day and St. Peter had only just woken up. He asked her whether she had considered the questions and she nodded in response.

"Well then "he said, "which two days of the week start with the letter 'T'?

The blonde woman said, "Today and Tomorrow."

St. Peter pondered the answer for some time and eventually decided that her answer was perfectly correct in every sense. He couldn't fault it, even though it had surprised him.

"Now, can I have your answer to the second question. How many seconds are there in a year?"

"Twelve!" she replied without hesitation.

"Only twelve," he said, "how can that be?"

"It's easy," she said. "There's the second of January, the second of February and so on right through to the second of December. Unless my maths are wrong, that makes twelve seconds."

St. Peter looked at her and wondered what on earth she was up to.

"I need some time to consider your answer before I can give you a decision," he said, and walked away scratching his head.

A short time later he returned. "I'll allow the answer to stand, but I need your solution to the third question before can go any further. It needs to be absolutely correct if you are to be allowed into Heaven. What is the name of the swagman in Waltzing Matilda?"

"Oh, that was the easiest of the three," she smiled winningly. "It's 'Andy.'

"Andy?" St. Peter was dubious.

"Of course," she said, but offered no explanation.

St. Peter paced up and down trying to work it out, but was defeated and he was forced to ask her how in God's name she had arrived at her answer.

"Easy," said the still smiling woman. 'Andy sat, Andy watched, Andy waited till his billy boiled."

St. Peter laughed and opened the Pearly gates wide in welcome, and as he did so a certain tune was threading its way through his head. I bet you're doing the same now, aren't you?

Owen Blatchly

THE TREASURER'S CHALLENGE – 2018

STRANGE TALES & COINCIDENCES OF MY FAMILY AND FRIENDS

In the late 1940's my paternal grandfather suffered a stroke from which he only partly recovered and, as a result of his unfortunate disability, he was confined to a sitting room for most of the day. There he would continue one of his pastimes, which was to read science books, and, often, medical books on the causes and outcome of the condition from which he was suffering. Sadly, eighteen years later at the age of 59, while getting out of bed in the early hours of the morning to relieve himself, he dropped dead. I'm told this is not an unusual occurrence for men of a certain age.

Strangely, his otherwise reliable Waltham pocket watch, which he always placed on the very substantial bedside table, stopped at the actual moment of his passing. My father (his son) left the watch set at the time he died for some years, and, in spite of much handling, it never got going again by itself.

About three weeks after the sad event, my father saw my grandfather sitting in his usual position on the settee in the living room, reading a book. He turned, smiled and disappeared. My father was prepared to concede that it may have been a 'ghost of the mind' in that he had been used to seeing his father in that position over many years.

After my grandmother also passed away, in nothing like such spectacular circumstances, the house was lived in by a middle aged couple, who later confessed to being sensitive to 'supernatural events.' At first they seemed happy there, but later admitted to collectively and individually hearing various unusual sounds and seeing the weight chandelier light fitting in the sitting room swinging erratically from side to side.

At this time, I was working with a practice in Truro, and one of my work colleagues had a wife who also claimed to be sensitive to the supernatural. I asked him if his wife would be prepared to help me out with a possible problem. In order not to generate any preconceptions I did not tell either the husband or the wife what it was about. The wife agreed to meet me at the property. By this time the tenants had vacated the house and I asked her if she could feel anything in the dwelling. She went from room to room on the ground floor saying 'nothing here', until we arrived at the doorway to my grandparents' upstairs bedroom where, without hesitation, she immediately pointed diagonally across the room and said 'there.' It was the precise spot where my grandfather had dropped dead over 50 years earlier and was the room above the sitting room where the former tenants claimed the strange events were taking place.

It is suggested that such events are caused by the souls of the departed who find themselves trapped between this world and the next, particularly if they suffered a violent or sudden death. The local woman said various prayers and incantations to try and release whoever it was, and I joined in enthusiastically, if with not a little skepticism. Whether we succeeded, I don't know. All I can say is that subsequent residents have not reported anything untoward since.

****

The village where I was brought up and from which both sides of my family originated did not have a mains water supply until well into the 1950s. For the majority who did not have their own wells, drinking water was obtained from one of the two local pumps in the village 'shute' (a pipe which projected out of a stone retaining wall) and was transported to the various houses in a beer barrel on a horse drawn vehicle, which was simply a frame with two wheels, by the local water carrier, a well-known and much loved character and his loyal pony

'Jessie'. A bucketful of water was one penny (1d) and a barrelful, if you were lucky enough to have the facility to store it, was two shillings and sixpence. (2/6d) Fortunately, my paternal grandparents were lucky enough to have the space for a round galvanized covered tank in a courtyard next to their side door that was reserved specifically for the purpose. The tank was conveniently situated in a courtyard next to the side door of their house. Almost at the bottom of the tank was a tap, the type with a square brass projection on top that fitted into a corresponding square hole in a removable key. Once the key had been taken off it was impossible to turn the tap on or off by hand and therefore impossible for someone to do it out of mischief. To prevent the latter in particular, my grandparents kept the key in a hole in an adjacent concrete block wall. Although my parents' house next door was, at that time, fortunate enough to have a plumbed-in 300-gallon rainwater tank for general household purposes, the drinking water supply was shared with my grandparents using a portable one-gallon water can with a lid and handle. This meant a 75 yard round trip every time we needed three kettlefuls of drinking water.

Nevertheless, jubilation arrived in about 1953 when eventually mains water arrived, not only supplying the village itself but also surrounding villages and rural areas. The source of water, however, was the main shaft of a local mine which had a reputation in the old mining days of being one of the most corrosive mines in Cornwall. Apparently the miners' leather boots would rot after only a few days of working in the wet underground conditions. Although the water was highly filtered and 'purified' my mother would not drink it, for the simple reason that the source was surrounded by her father's farm, and she knew from first- hand experience that he and other local farmers, disposed of their dead cattle down the disused shaft. Furthermore, and what she considered worse, a villager was last seen heading in that direction never to be seen again and it was suspected that he took his own life by throwing himself down the open shaft. In short, there was no way my mother was going to drink the new mains water and so we continued with the old system for many years until the Stithians Dam had been constructed and the mine source had been discontinued.

In 1960 my grandmother, like her husband, suffered a stroke and had to leave the home that meant so much to her, to be taken into care and where she eventually died eighteen months later; her house remaining empty during her absence. One evening, about three weeks after her death, my father went to refill the drinking water container from the tank in his mother's courtyard. He placed the container under the tap and before he could reach for the key in the wall, the tap turned on full-bore filling the can to the brim. This had never happened before or since. Father had to use the key to turn it off but could give no explanation for this strange incident, except that it was Granny letting us know that everything was okay with her!

****

In the early 1930s after leaving school, my father joined a firm of Newquay estate agents with the aim of eventually becoming an architect. However, like so many of his generation, Herr Hitler put a stop to that, although he remained in the building industry as a building surveyor, leaving it to the next generation to create the carbuncles! As was common in those days, the company he worked for were also auctioneers and on this particular occasion my father and a colleague were sent to a house by the name of 'Eveningside' on the western side of Mount Wise, where an elderly lady had recently died. It was the duty of the pair to catalogue the old lady's effects and create lots for the forthcoming sale.

My father decided to sort out the contents of one of the first floor bedrooms, which included a selection of books piled up on a table in the room, while his colleague dealt with other matters downstairs. Father went into the room, closed the door the door and sat down at the table to perform his task. After a few minutes he heard the door click open. He found this a little irritating and, thinking that he hadn't closed it properly, he got up and close it again. He made sure that this time the latch was secure. He then returned to his chore. Minutes later the door opened again. He shut it again, satisfying himself that there was no wind or draught that could cause it to open. Needless to say, it happened again. This time his curiosity got the better of him and he closed the door securely, stepped back and watched. A few moments had passed when he saw the doorknob turn and the door clicked open. Father grabbed the doorknob expecting to see his colleague on the other side playing a trick on him. His colleague was downstairs getting on with his work. There was no one in sight. My father then called his colleague to witness what was going on, which he did. The knob turned while they were both watching and the door opened. Somewhat uneasily father continued his work, but left the door wide open. I do not know whether anything else occurred.

The contents of 'Eveningside' were auctioned and eventually the house itself was sold. By chance, some friends of our family purchased the property, quite unaware of my father's earlier experience. Before moving in our friends had some alterations made. These included the installation of a bathroom, which the house previously did not possess. To enable this improvement, the door which had been so troublesome had been bricked up and another formed in a different position. These friends, consisting of elderly parents and two unmarried daughters came to my parents' house to dinner one evening in early January, as part of the Christmas celebrations. They had just moved from 'Eveningside' to a new house in West Pentire. It seems quite clear that for some reason they didn't stay at 'Eveningside' very long. As they were no longer connected with the house, my father mentioned quizzically, "I understand that Eveningside is haunted. Furtive glances went around the table.

After a short silence the younger sister blurted "You know that Ken is correct – it is!" She then divulged that early during their occupation of the property she went to the new bathroom to run the hot water for the bath, where she was wearing only her bathrobe. While waiting for the bath to fill a 'force' grabbed the collar of her bathrobe behind her neck and whipped the garment off her. It scared her so much that from then on she would not take a bath without her older sister being present.

Eventually the family discovered that, in the mid-19th century when the house was being built, there was a decorator painting the walls in the stairwell from a ladder perched on the staircase. Apparently, the ladder slipped and the decorator fell to an instant death. Once again a sudden or violent death seems to have been the cause.

If I am correct I think the house has since been demolished and the site redeveloped. Whether the 'ghost' was carried away with the rubble or is still there, who knows?

****

My great, great, great grandmother, Harriet T, who at the time of this story was elderly and suffered from poor sight and hearing, was a devout Christian of Methodist persuasion. She lived at Mithian Downs to the east of Blackwater, and would regularly walk along a network of narrow lanes and footpaths to attend Services and Prayer Meetings at one of the chapels in Chacewater, a distance of some four miles each way. Her route took her across the un-manned level crossing over the main railway line at Jolly's Bottom.

At that time, it is probable that the main line from Truro to Penzance was still only single track. At this point on the line it was fairly straight to the west with a clear view toward the viaducts and Chacewater Station about a mile distant, but to the east, on the Truro side, was a sharp bend in a deep cutting.

On one particular summer morning Harriet was making the crossing when she suddenly became aware of an approaching train. Because of her poor sight and hearing it seems she became very confused, not being sure of which way the train was approaching and whether she had just stepped onto the track or off it. Whatever, she was struck by the train coming around the bend from the Truro direction, hurled some distance and (thankfully) killed instantly. She was subsequently buried at Mithian Churchyard.

In late August 1987, one of my father's second cousins, Lambert T, (both being great, great grandsons of Harriet) came home on holiday to the UK from Australia to visit his surviving relatives. On Monday 29th August my parents invited him to tea. However, because he was helping my mother to prepare for Lambert's visit, father did not do what he usually did on a Monday morning. Nevertheless, Lambert duly arrived and during the afternoon's conversation the matter of family history was addressed, a subject which Lambert was deeply into; so much so that he had brought with him what appeared to be reams of hard copies of persons bearing the 'T 'family surname (and the many variants thereof) obtained from the Mormon Church in Salt Lake City that specialised in compiling family names globally.

As the conversation went on, Lambert asked my father whether he knew the date when their great, great grandmother, Harriet, was killed on the railway line, as it would give him clues to further information. As I was present, I recall father replying, 'it was certainly before my day, and as far as I am aware before my mother's day, too'. The conversation continued, tea was served and eventually after a pleasant afternoon, Lambert left to return to his sister's house where he was staying.

The next morning, Tuesday, father did what he normally did on Monday morning, that is to read the local newspaper – 'The Argus'. This paper was a small tabloid issued by the West Briton with circulation limited to the Truro area, and which has long since been discontinued. Included in the 'Argus' was a 'Looking Back' section with extracts of events that happened 25 years ago, 50 years ago, and 100 years ago. Although, for the 100-year period, the article in the 1987 Argus was summarised, the full report in the Monday Evening Edition of the West Briton of August 29th 1887, from which the following was taken, reads:

Fatal Accident near Chacewater – Yesterday morning, (Sunday 28th August) when approaching Chacewater, the engine driver of the train due at Penzance at 10.45am observed a woman on the line. He sounded the whistle, shut off steam, reversed gear, and did all he could to avert an accident but the unfortunate woman – who is elderly, and is either deaf or was absorbed in thought – was knocked down and run over. An arm and a leg were smashed, and she was otherwise so injured that when the train was stopped and guards and passengers went back, she was found to be dead. Her name is Mrs. T, and she resided near Chacewater.

It appears that it was exactly 100 years to within a day, that Harriet's great, Great grandsons were discussing the date of her death from when it actually happened. It made the hairs on the back of our necks stand on end! As well as being able to provide Lambert with the information he required, father contacted the

West Briton Journalist concerned, with the story of this strange 'coincidence', and which she published the following week!

****

In the late 19th Century and early 20^{th,} one of my great grandfathers on my mother's side, farmed the land at Mount Pleasant, Threemilestone, where Richard Lander School and much of the residential development to the west now stands. One winter Wednesday, he attended Truro Cattle Market, presumably in good health, completed his business and left the market for home in his horse drawn 'jingle' (or governess cart). The horse arrived home safely after dark, with its passenger stone -dead in the jingle. This was obviously a great shock to his family. Presumably great grandfather died from a heart attack or stroke. The horse obviously knew its way home!

****

Directly after my grandmother died my father let her house to a portrait painter Stanley B and his wife Jess. They had been living elsewhere in the village for some time, having moved down to Cornwall from the Southeast, and were looking for somewhere bigger. About midway through their 25 year stay, Stan's uncle, who was also then living in the London area, decided that he wanted to move to the village to be nearer his nephew and his wife. This he did and 'Uncle Bert' moved to a small rented 'two up and two down' terraced cottage conveniently just five doors along the road from his relatives. After about ten years, Uncle Bert's health deteriorated and he passed away peacefully. It was left to his nephew and niece-in-law to sort out his effects and to clean the cottage to hand back to the landlord. However,

Stan himself was not well, leaving the onerous task to Jess alone. Appreciating the situation that Jess found herself in, my mother offered her services of help, and so one evening they both sallied forth armed with brushes, dustpans, buckets and cloths to give the property a good clean-through. As the evening moved on it was necessary to put the electric lights on. Nevertheless, while Jess and mother were working the lights inexplicably went out. After a few seconds they came on again. After about thirty seconds they went off again, and while they were off Jess said, 'Come on Uncle Bert stop messing about!' and the lights came on again.

Whether Jess was being serious I can't recall – somehow I think she was. However, my mother, being of a somewhat nervous disposition, was scared stiff and Jess had to take her home. To make matters worse, although the properties were on the same electricity supply, my father confirmed that to his knowledge there had not been a power cut in my parents' house at that time. Sorry to say, Jess had to complete her task alone.

A few years later, it was my mother's turn to cast off her mortal coil, leaving my father on his own. In order to help with the transition of being without mother, my wife and I decided to stay with him on alternate nights for about the first month or so. On one particular evening (again about three weeks after mother had passed away), my wife and I had already booked to take the children to see an evening performance at the Minack Theatre, which we subsequently fulfilled, arriving back at my father's late in the evening.

It was my wife's turn to stay on this particular night and so I dropped her at my father's gate, made sure she was in the house, and drove our half-asleep children back to our home. When my wife went into the house the downstairs hall and upstairs landing lights were on, and though father was awake he had switched his bedroom light off. My wife went into the spare room, the door of which was directly opposite that of my father's, switched the bedroom light on and the hall and landing lights off. She then changed into her nightdress and dressing gown, went into father's room, sat down on a chair inside the door with the only lighting shining across the landing from the spare bedroom where she was going to sleep. She then gave an account to father of the evening's happenings at the Minack.

While they were talking the landing light went 'on' and after a pause it went 'off'. Following a short interval, the process was repeated. There was no one else in the house, no one was near to the light switches, and when my wife checked the light switches afterwards there was nothing untoward about them. The conclusion they came to was that it was mother making some form of contact informing us that everything was OK. My mother wasn't a very inventive lady, and we surmised that what was a good enough means of communication for 'Uncle Bert' was good enough her!

****

I was born at Newquay in 1941, and for the first eleven years of my life I was brought up there. In those days Sundays were very different from what they are today. No organised sports or superstores and Sunday shopping. Although in the summertime, following Chapel Service and Sunday School in the morning, we would naturally gravitate towards the beach in the afternoon (when strangely the weather always seemed to be hot and sunny); during the other three seasons we would go on family Sunday afternoon walks. One of my parents' favourite jaunts was to cross the River Gannel at low tide by one of the two little timber footbridges onto the Crantock side, walk along the coastal footpath and have afternoon tea, or in my case an ice cream soda, at a genteel tearoom run by two elderly (or that's what they seemed to be to me then!) ladies in their 1930s bungalow overlooking the beautiful Gannel estuary.

After crossing the bridge, on the Crantock side of the river, was Penpol Creek (yes there is more than one!) where sat, partly buried in the sand, an old black hulk that had been moored there prior to my arrival on the planet and which we, as school children, affectionately knew as the 'Skoo-neraydah'.   She was in fact a two-masted 98ft long sailing schooner 'The Ada' built in Barrow-in-Furness in the 19th century that mainly worked around Cornish and other British ports carrying coal probably from South Wales. In the mid- 1930s, at the end of her working life, the ship was purchased privately and brought up the Gannel, moored at Penpol Creek and became a houseboat and small museum exhibiting the private collection of items acquired by the ship's owner. This proved to be a great attraction to visitors to Newquay in those days.

In 1951, when she got beyond being maintained in a watertight condition, the Ada's pitch pine decks were salvaged and the rest of this iconic old ship was sadly and ceremoniously torched.   I understand that she burned for two weeks. The old schooner was then replaced by a redundant WWII motor torpedo boat – renamed 'The Ada' in memory of her predecessor. When the second boat reached scrapping stage, the museum collection was transferred to the now preserved 'Trenance Cottages' in Newquay, and 'Ada' number two presumably suffered a similar fate to her namesake. Nevertheless, like Ronnie Corbett in his chair, I digress – but hopefully having given the reader a little bit of history of one of Cornwall's little beauty spots.

Leaving the 'Ada' behind us we then had to scramble up some roughly hewn steps in the coastal rocks to reach the narrow footpath which led us to Crantock. After a few yards, to the left and just before a steep rise in the footpath, was a small disused quarry grown-in with brambles and other impenetrable vegetation, and to the right was a hedge and then the river.   As a child I didn't like the quarry. I found it rather 'spooky' to say the least and was always pleased when I had walked up out of the rise in the footpath into the open field beyond. In my later teens I put the 'spookiness' down to vivid childhood imaginations. I changed my mind in my mid-twenties when my future wife and I were invited to a party hosted by mutual Newquay friends.   The condition of accepting the party invitation was that each guest had to be armed with a 'ghost story'.   I can't remember which story I told, nor that of my fiancé, but I vividly recollect the one told by another of the guests.

The story was that a local Newquay chap, with whom the story teller was acquainted, had at that time a girlfriend who lived in Crantock. After taking her home one evening he returned along the Gannel footpath just as it was getting dusk. As he was walking along the open section of footpath in the field towards the disused quarry, no doubt deep in thought, another chap came out of the rise which concealed the quarry and walked towards him. As the footpath was only one person wide the first chap stood to one side onto the grass to allow the second to pass. As the latter passed, the former said 'Good evening' to him. There was no reply. Thinking the passerby to be rude and discourteous, the first chap turned his head to make some comment to the figure retreating towards Crantock only to discover that there was no one there!! I imagine the walker ran back to Newquay as quickly as he could.

In the 1990s I related the above strange story to a friend, Robin, who had joined my practice as a member of staff. Robin immediately replied and said that he had had a very similar experience at the same location. In his case he too was walking back from Crantock in the dusk to Newquay to his parents,' who were then living on the West Pentire side overlooking the Gannel and could see the old quarry in the distance from their windows. In Robin's case, as he was walking along the footpath towards the open field, he saw another figure walking ahead of him. Being a somewhat lonely place, Robin wanted to keep the person in his sight so he increased his pace and kept the other person in view – that is until Robin lost sight of him as the other person disappeared into the dip before the quarry. Although Robin continued along the path, strangely he did not catch even a glimpse of the other 'person' again! The only explanation I have heard for this phenomenon is that some time ago, presumably around or before WWII, someone drowned in the dangerously strong tidal current while swimming off the small point opposite the quarry where Penpol Creek meets the main flow of the Gannel. Nevertheless, during the second World War American GIs were based in the woods around Penpol Creek. Whether it was one of them who met their sad demise there, while being foolhardy, who knows? If this is the case, then once again it seems to be the outcome of an unexpected and sudden tragic death.

****

The latter story was not the only one Robin had to relate. The next one apparently occurred one summer evening in about 1975, when he had just driven from working in another part of Cornwall. The time was approximately 6.30pm, His father had a responsible position on the railway, and the house was located close to it. Robin parked his car in the railway station yard near some steps that led to a little white gate in the railings between the station yard and the road. As he went through the gate and turned to lock it, he by chance glanced up over the railway tracks to the countryside beyond the town, when he noticed a large white sphere in the sky and wondered what it was. As he was looking at it, the sphere started to drift in his direction over the town's river and railway lines and seemed very low in the sky. It then stopped and hovered above him. Robin then noticed that there seemed to be no vehicular activity on the nearby road and no people present. There was a strange calm and stillness; everything seemed silent throughout the experience and he felt quite alone. Robin found the occurrence, which seemed to last for several minutes, most disconcerting. During this time, he stood looking up at the sphere still trying to work out what it was. It then started to move away over the station yard and car park toward the railway lines and the bridge over the town's river in the direction of its estuary. As it did so the sphere rose into the sky, became much smaller and disappeared. Robin then walked to the house wondering what it was that he had just witnessed.

He was convinced that it was definitely not a weather balloon or remotely anything of human design. It was more like a mini planet or moon and was completely silent. Robin is of the type to seek a logical explanation for such a phenomenon. As far as he recalls, once the sphere had disappeared and the event was over, normal traffic and people activity resumed. Robin then recorded his experience in a book that contained other matters of importance. Strangely he has never been able to find that book since!

****

Robin's next story relates to experiences he had in the same family home that he has referred to previously. During the long period his family occupied the house and when he was sleeping in the front bedroom, Robin would often be awakened feeling something walking over his bedclothes, it was not particularly heavy, but he definitely felt a walking motion. Sometimes when he plucked up the courage he would jump up to see what it was but there was nothing there, and sometimes it would return very soon afterwards. He ruled out the possibility of it being a pet cat or any other animal. On one occasion he moved to the larger back bedroom, which gave him more space. The room had previously been used as a spare bedroom or just a spare room, as necessary. From this bedroom was an access door to a back staircase that led to the roof attic where the water tank and electricity meter were located. In spite of the increase in space he did not stay in that room for very long. He experienced very strange and uncomfortable happenings and feelings which were difficult to describe or explain. He eventually returned to the front bedroom (being the lesser of the two 'evils').

The house still exists but Robin understands it has been converted into two self-contained flats. However sometime later Robin's parents confessed to him that they also had sightings of a male figure in the kitchen and on the staircase and they were not the sort of people to make up false stories.

****

Robin's final story again involves the same family house. After 30 years occupying it, Robin's father retired and the family decided to move elsewhere. While making preparations, his mother went upstairs to her bedroom. Robin and his father were downstairs in the kitchen and heard a loud chilling scream. It was his mother who then called them to quickly come up. Robin ran upstairs to find his mother in a state of shock and extremely upset as she pointed to her bedroom. Robin opened the door and entered wondering what he was about to find. All the bits and pieces on his mother's dressing table and the bedroom mantelpiece had been knocked to the floor. There were no windows open and there was no draught. Robin then went out onto the landing and his mother said that as she was getting ready she felt something in the room and that all of a sudden her bits and pieces were knocked off her dressing table and the mantel shelf. She did not see or hear anything, just the noise of the objects falling onto the floor. When the matter was discussed between them later, they wondered if the 'presence' referred to above was objecting to them leaving the house as they had been living there so long.

Anon.

THAT'S RICH

A boat docked in a tiny fishing village in Cornwall and a wealthy looking tourist asked the fisherman how long it took him to catch his fish.

"Not long," answered the Cornishman.

"So why don't you stay out longer and catch more?" asked the tourist

The Cornishman explained his small catch was sufficient to meet his needs and those of his family, but the tourist was not giving up.

"What do you do with the rest of your time?"

"I sleep late, fish a little, play with my children and take a siesta with my wife. In the evenings I go to the village pub and see my friends, have a few drinks and we sing a few songs. I have a full life."

The tourist interrupted. "I have a business degree and I can help you. You should start by fishing longer every day. You could then sell the extra fish you catch. With the extra income you can buy a bigger boat. With the extra money the larger boat will bring, you can buy a second and a third and so on until you have a fleet of trawlers. Instead of selling your fish to a middle man, you can negotiate directly with the processing plants and maybe open your own plant. You can then leave this village and move to a large city and from there direct your enterprise."

The tourist was pleased with his lesson in economics and awaited a response.

"How long would that take?" asked the fisherman.

"Oh, 20 or possibly 25 years," replied the tourist.

"And after that?"

That's when it gets really interesting," answered the businessman. "When your business gets really big, you can sell stocks and shares and make millions."

"Millions? And then what?"

THE TREASURER'S CHALLENGE – 2018

"After that, you'll be able to retire, live in a tiny village near the coast, sleep late, play with your children, catch a few fish, take a siesta with your wife, and spend the evenings in the pub drinking and singing with your friends."

Paul Stuart

THE TREASURER'S CHALLENGE – 2018

<u>MY FRIEND AMBER</u>

I sense something is going on. I was up awakened from my slumbers last night and watched over my friend Amber, who was stretched out on the kitchen floor breathing the deepest of breaths. We are friends and have been for many a year, ever since I first arrived and she took me under her wing and made me feel at home. We have done a lot of things together, Amber and I. We kept a vigil for three long nights and three long days when our much loved master was leaving us. He left us far too soon. He hadn't done nearly all of the things on his to do list, but we don't have much choice in the matter, something we understand much better than our humans, who seem to try and live forever.

Our home was picked up and we were taken to somewhere else to live, which was a long way away. I liked it, but Amber was homesick until she made some friends. I don't need friends.

But something was afoot. I saw my mistress kneel on the floor and whisper to Amber, who lifted her poor tired head a little bit and wagged her tail before sinking back down again. I sat and waited. Some other humans came and sat in the conservatory and then Ewan turned up and they sat some more, talking softly. Amber lay in the garage where it was cool and she was happiest. And I waited.

Eventually, nice Mr. Vet arrived with a lady carrying stuff. I don't know what it was. Amber staggered to her feet and wagged her tail and they said "are you sure?" My mistress nodded and when nice Mr. Vet watched how Amber had to be helped up the steps, he said, "Yes, you're right. It is time."

They all came into the conservatory. The sun was shining and it was time for my morning sleep, but I had to stay. Ewan and my mistress knelt and took Amber in their arms and held her close. And then she was gone.

Just like that. She was gone. I watched and waited and then I padded over to where she lay and I breathed all around her head and her face, and her beautiful brown eyes, which were slowly closing. I said goodbye to Amber.

And now I am top cat. I rule. I sleep on the bed, I have caught two mice which I presented to my mistress and I jump on her head every morning at five o'clock demanding breakfast. Life is good. I am a cat and I am wise enough to know that life goes on.

Judy McCavana

THE TREASURER'S CHALLENGE – 2018

<u>LOSS</u>

Throughout my career as a nurse, spanning over 40 years, I have witnessed loss many, many times. Sometimes it has involved families and, on other occasions, there has been no family presence at all.

You would imagine it to be a little easier to deal with if relatives were absent, but it wasn't.

I recall that quite early in my career a young boy was brought in from a 'school for naughty boys,' requiring stitches for a cut on his wrist. He had visited us many times before needing stitching up, and he always pulled them out himself before the wound had properly healed. This time I chatted to him at length, explaining that the wound would open and become infected if he were to remove them too soon. He promised that as long as I took them out for him, he would leave them in place until I removed them a week later. We arranged a date and time for the following week, when I was to be on duty. A couple of days later we had a call to say that there had been a fire and the ambulance was bringing a body to the department for us to certify. The fire had taken place in a hay barn. Some boys were smoking there and they had accidently set fire to the hay. The flames spread so quickly that their exit was blocked. There was a metal grill over the window which the fire brigade eventually managed to remove and several firemen had to be treated for burns to the hands. Myself and a doctor met the ambulance. The body bag contained the charred remains of a small person. My little friend would not be coming back to have his stitches removed.

Over the years I have remembered this tragic loss of young life with no family to mourn him, So sad.

Dealing with families is also very difficult. No two deaths are ever the same and people react very differently. You almost have to wait to be guided by the bereaved. Study days and training days don't really help. I feel you have to learn something from each experience and it's often best just to be there to listen and respond accordingly. There are, however, certain formalities that have to be dealt with and that requires sensitivity.

Having my faith has certainly helped me over the years and continues to do so, although I would be wrong if I said I never questioned it. Despite dealing with sadness and grief over the years, and, believe me, it was often incredibly emotional it did not prepare me for the emotions I felt for my own personal loss later in life.

I lost my own mother on Christmas Day, 2011, which was her 81st birthday, and my world as I had known it fell apart. Only through the love of my husband, Tim, and my children, Rebecca and Matthew, did I actually survive my grief. Owen Blatchly will probably never realise what an important part he played in helping me. We have always attended church, not regularly, but since coming to Perranarworthal I feel as though we have discovered a new family of friends and I look forward to our Sunday mornings.

I am going to include two pieces of work by other people. The first sums up how I felt after losing my dear Mum and are the words of Thomas More after his father's death: To Thomas Cromwell, 1530.

"He was the light of my life, my father.
We are not great men, we are a shadow of what they were.
It's strange, Thomas, but since he went, I feel my age.
As if I were just a boy, till a few days ago. But God has snapped his fingers and I see all my best years behind me."

The second is a very uplifting piece contributed by Sir Richard Branson to help to raise money for MIND.

"You don't know me but I hear you are going through a tough time, and I would like to help you. I want to be open and honest with you, and let you know that happiness isn't something just afforded to a special few. It can be yours, if you take time to let it grow.

It's okay to be stressed, scared and sad. I certainly have been throughout my 66 years. I've confronted my biggest fears time and time again. I've cheated death on many adventures and had my heart broken.

I know I'm fortunate to live an extraordinary life, and that most people would assume my business success and the wealth that comes with it, have brought me happiness. But they haven't; in fact, it's the reverse. I am successful, wealthy and connected because I am happy.

So many people get caught up in doing what they think will make them happy but, in my opinion, this is where they fail. Happiness is not about doing, it's about being. In order to be happy, you need to think consciously about it. Don't forget the to-do list, but remember to write a to-be list too.

Kids are often asked, 'what do you want to be when you grow up?' The world expects grandiose aspirations: 'I want to be a writer, a doctor, the Prime Minister.' They are told. 'go to school, go to college, get a job, get married and then you'll be happy.' But that's about doing, not being and while doing will bring you moments of joy it won't necessarily reward you with lasting happiness.

Stop and breathe. Be healthy. Be around your friends and family. Be there for someone, and let someone be there for you. Be bold. Just for a minute.

If you allow yourself to be in the moment, happiness will follow. I speak from experience. We've built a business empire, joined conversations about the future of our planet, attended many memorable parties and met many unforgettable people. And while these things have brought me great joy, it's the moments that I stopped just to be, rather than do, that have given me true happiness. Why? Because allowing yourself just to be, puts things into perspective. Try it. Be still. Be present.

For me, it's watching the flamingos fly across Necker Island at dusk. It's holding my new grandchild's tiny hands. It's looking up at the stars and dreaming of seeing them up close one day. It's listening to my family's dinner time debates. It's the smile on a stranger's face, the smell of rain, the ripple of a wave, the wind across the sand. It's the first snow fall of winter, and the last storm of summer. It's sunrise and sunset.

There's a reason we're called human beings and not human doings. As human beings we have the ability to think, move and communicate in a heightened way. We can co-operate, understand, reconcile and love. That's what sets us apart from most other species. Don't waste your human talents by stressing about nominal things, or that which you cannot change. If you take the time simply to be and appreciate the fruits of life, your stresses will begin to dissolve, and you will be happier.

But don't just seek happiness when you're down. Happiness shouldn't be a goal; it should be a habit. Take the focus off doing, and start by being every day. Be loving, be grateful, be helpful and be a spectator to your own thoughts. Allow yourself to be in the moment and appreciate the moment. Take the focus off everything you think you need to do and start being. I promise you, happiness will follow."

Lorraine Rogers.

<u>THE DOCTOR'S HANDS</u>

I often marvel at our creation. At how we can take for granted the incredible process that has created us. One day I was struck by the wonder of my hands and what they do in everyday life. I wrote the following in response to this thought and as homage to God's creation.

At that moment in time, optimistic bright sunlight through the window illuminated the sun tanned warmth of his right hand. He looked down and observed the wonderful shape and structure, remembering his mother's word just after his father had died.

"You have your father's hands."

Now, as everything stopped silently and the world around him withdrew, he focused to enjoy the utter peace of contemplation. As if in a trance, a wave of child-like wonder warmed him with a sense of gratitude.

How we communicate with our hands.

The greeting: a hand outstretched reaches out to grasp another. The firm grip of strength, honour, welcome. Not a limp, weak cold, moist grip that his father said was "like shaking hands with a wet fish."

Affection: The flat firm protective strength passing through the friend's back in a hug.

Love: The first time his sensitive fingers entwined between the small cold fingers of his love as they walked obliviously alone in the country. How the transmitted intimacy of touch tingled in the pit of his stomach as she stroked his palm with her thumb. Later, the softness of caress and the first realization of soft, smooth feminine skin that never ceases to marvel.

The Doctor: The patient sits anxious with anticipation, slightly upright, looking forward. He would stop and listen to the history and then take a moment to take the pulse. Perhaps no longer so important, but to him a chance to feel the life force through his fingers, the quickened pace of anxiety, fever, the irregularity of cardiac problems, the weakness of failing health.

A time to think quietly, inwardly. To withdraw and enjoy the quiet cloak of contemplation like the moment sunlight fell onto his hand.

Later, examining the abdomen as the patient lies on his couch, he remembers those early anatomy lessons, picturing the inner organs. Slowly feeling. Starting on the left lower side and gently moving around. Looking down, watching the way his strong fingers pressed gently into the flesh. Not in the way so many doctors he observed do, in a forceful, pushing fashion and the eyes of the patient look frightened, distressed but resigned.

He never felt the need for that.

Information passed through his fingers and into his mind all the time as he contemplated the problem. As he took the blood pressure, his hands squeezed the rubber bulb, moving in a rhythm, with strength. He thought of his strong grip as he used a chisel, gripping the smooth boxwood handle, pushing hard into the wood, watching the wonderful honey coloured shavings falling away to drop curled onto the bench. He pictured the John Everett Millais painting of 'Christ in the House of his Parents.' He felt himself holding the smooth handle of an awl pushing firmly through leather, watching the tension in the knuckle gripping the handle. How the smooth head fits in the palm. Marveling how hand axes from the stone age are all the same size wherever they are found in the world, created with skill. The slow and careful knapping of flint shards. The mind thinking, watching and the hand moving the shaped stone slowly emerging from the rock.

The patient dresses, sits, again upright, anxious and holding the questions back, looking at his eyes as he looks down to record his thoughts. The doctor reaches for a pen. It is smooth, black and fits perfectly in his hand. He likes the way the ink flows secretly from the nib and the small flash of warm gold, just like the sunlight. He watches the letters form, not always the shape he imagines in his mind. He pictures the beautiful shaped writing of long ago. There is a sense of peace again, a moment of quiet thought as he observes the gentle way his fingers grip and hold the pen so delicately.

Sitting back, he folds his hands, the fingers entwined in a personal caress. His eyes meet those of the patient. Reassurance, explanation and he watches him relax and slightly melt back from the tense pose. He observes the change in posture, the way the eyes begin to smile again.

Explanation, resting his chin on his crossed fingers. The moment is passing.

A final word to ensure the questions have been aired, the doubt gone. The space between them closes. He gets up, walks closer and shakes a hand. An unsaid feeling of gratitude passes between them as the door is opened and he says goodbye. A final touch as the firm cupping fingers close on the passing shoulder. The final touch of human reassurance.

Tim Rogers

#0041 - 200818 - C0 - 229/152/6 [8] - CB - DID2280405